Grace for Grace

Grace for Grace

WATCHMAN NEE

Translated from the Chinese

Christian Fellowship Publishers, Inc.
New York

ISBN 0-935008-59-4

Available from the Publishers at:

11515 Allecingie Parkway
Richmond, Virginia 23235

PRINTED IN U.S.A.

TRANSLATOR'S PREFACE

"And the Word became flesh, and dwelt among us . . . full of grace and truth" (John 1.14). This tells us of what Christ Jesus is as He came to tabernacle among men. "For of his fulness we all received, and grace for grace" (John 1.16). This shows us what happens to us after we receive Him. "Grace for grace"—this is the blessed portion of all who receive Christ. In the words of George Hutcheson, it is "grace upon grace, grace after grace, and more grace because we have already been given grace." "Each blessing appropriated," wrote B. W. Westcott, "became the foundation of a greater blessing. To have realized and used one measure of grace was to have gained a larger measure (as it were) in exchange for it."

In this present volume Watchman Nee first presents to us the series of parables dealing with the new and the old, together with the parable of the prodigal son, in order to illustrate what the grace is that we have received. He then proceeds to show what grace does to us as seen in the blood of Jesus which speaks better than that of Abel, to show the relationship between sin and the body, the meaning of baptism, and also the benefits of confessing sin. Finally, he puts forward what grace does in us as demonstrated in our desire to have communion with God and in our love of God, with the story of Mary Magdalene serving as the natural conclusion to the entire book.

May we bow and worship the Lord of grace.

CONTENTS

This volume consists of messages delivered by the author over an extended period of anointed ministry of God's word. Because of the relatedness of their content, they are now being translated and published in English as a single volume.

Scripture quotations are from the
American Standard Version of the Bible
(1901), unless otherwise indicated.

1 | Parables of the New and the Old

And after these things he went forth, and behold a publican, named Levi, sitting at the place of toll, and said unto him, Follow me. And he forsook all, and rose up and followed him. . . . And Jesus answering said unto them, They that are in health have no need of a physician; but they that are sick. I am not come to call the righteous but sinners to repentance. . . . And he spake also a parable unto them: No man rendeth a piece from a new garment and putteth it upon an old garment; else he will rend the new, and also the piece from the new will not agree with the old. And no man putteth new wine into old wine-skins; else the new wine will burst the skins, and itself will be spilled, and the skins will perish. But new wine must be put into fresh wine-skins. And no man having drunk old desireth new; for he saith, The old is good. (Luke 5.27–39)

. . . And no man putteth a piece of undressed cloth upon an old garment; for that which should fill it up taketh it from the garment, and a worse rent is made.

> Neither do men put new wine into old wine-skins: else the skins burst, and the wine is spilled, and the skins perish: but they put new wine into fresh wine-skins, and both are preserved. (Matt. 9.9–17)

Once when the Lord traveled and came to a certain place, He saw Matthew (Levi) sitting at the customs. He called Levi, saying, "Follow me," and the latter arose and followed the Lord. Suppose a stranger would say to us, "Follow me"; would we rise up and follow him? Certainly not. But here is a Man to whom Matthew is drawn as iron to a magnet: he cannot help but forsake his former life, wealth and all, and follow Him. Who knows the power behind Jesus' word that causes Matthew to renounce his sinful life and abandon everything? Here is a Man that whoever sees Him must repent and be saved, that whoever listens to His voice will receive a new life, that whoever hears His call will rise up and follow Him.

Now after Matthew had answered the Lord's call, he prepared a banquet that he might entertain Jesus. At the same time he also invited many publicans and sinners to come and eat with them. While they were at the table eating, certain Pharisees and their scribes murmured. They could not understand why the Lord Jesus and His disciples would have liked to eat and drink with publicans and sinners! They dared not question the Lord face to face, so they complained to His disciples, saying, "Why do ye eat and drink with the publicans and sinners?" The disciples could not answer them, perhaps because they themselves did not understand why their Master would do such a thing. When the Lord Jesus heard about it, He replied: "I am not come to call the righteous (ones) but sinners to repentance." This is the purpose of His coming to the world. He does not compromise himself in the least by attending a banquet in a publican's home, nor does He by chance eat with publicans and sinners. He comes with a definite aim. He says "I am not . . . but." This explains the reason for His coming. His incarnation is specially motivated. Whether He walks or He heals, it is full of meaning. He never does anything casually nor does He say anything carelessly. His whole life is disciplined. And hence, what He said here meant the following: You thought I communicated with the publicans and sinners because I was invited to eat with them; actually *this* is the motive of my coming from heaven: I am come that I might call sinners to repentance. I am come for this very purpose, and I have not changed My original plan.

Reason for the Parables

"They that are in health have no need of a physician; but they that are sick," observes the Lord. Why does He say this? Because many people do not understand the purpose of the law. We should know that God gives the law not for men to keep but rather for them to know that they cannot keep it. "What then is the law? It was added," declares the Scripture, "because of transgressions" (Gal. 3.19a). God already knows men have sinned, and yet people themselves do not know they have sinned. So God gives the law in order to cause men to know themselves and to know that they cannot keep the law. Surely our Lord knows all about this. It is absolutely inconceivable that the Son of God would come to this world to teach people to keep the law which is beyond their power to keep and which is itself added because of transgression. Since the law cannot keep people from sinning, would the Son of God come to tell them to do the impossible? God sends His Son to save men, therefore the Son will not insist on their keeping the law as a condition for their salvation.

God sends His Son to the world that the world might be saved through Him. We are all sick people. How, then, will God deal with us? He has two steps. First, He causes us to know that we are sick; and second, He induces us to ask for a physician. Suppose, for example, that a person has tuberculosis but he will not acknowledge it. He argues, How can I have tuberculosis when I am rather stout? You try to convince him by saying that his daily symptoms seem to indicate he has tuberculosis in the first stage, and that if he fails to seek out healing now, he will not be easily cured when the disease becomes more serious. Nevertheless, he insists that he does not have tuberculosis. Is it that because he denies he has tuberculosis he will not have tuberculosis? Not at all. His denial only indicates that he refuses to acknowledge that he has it. With the result that the tuberculosis in such a person will eventually become incurable.

The same is true with our salvation. The problem

is not because God has no way to save us; the problem lies instead in people's not knowing and acknowledging that they are sinners. For this reason, God first gives the law to men to cause them to see that they are indeed sinners. The law gives us the knowledge of sin; it also causes us to know ourselves. But the law cannot ever make us just, nor can it save us.

The order of salvation, therefore, is first, God gives us the law, and then He sends the Lord Jesus as grace to the world. When a physician examines a patient, he first diagnoses the disease and next he writes out a prescription. God gives the law that people might know they are sinners; He then sends grace—that is, He sends the Lord Jesus—that they might be healed. To those who are so stiff-necked as to say they are not sick, that they have no sin, to them the Lord Jesus declares: "I am not come to call the righteous (the self-righteous people)." What He means to say here is this: "I will have to let you self-righteous people continue to keep the law and be Pharisees." People must receive the first help before they can receive the second. If they are not willing to accept the witness of the law, they will not be able to receive the help of grace and truth. Formerly I thought I was fine; but the physician, after he has felt my pulse and measured my temperature and carefully examined me, tells me I am a sick man. Formerly I considered myself a good man, but now I meet the law which tells me I am a sinner. The work of the law is to show people that they are sick with sin.

"They that are in health have no need of a physician; but they that are sick." This is a basic principle.

Are you sick? Do you have some hidden illness you will not tell others about? Do you have in your heart some secret sins which are undetected by men? Let me say outright that God knows all hidden illness and secret sins. He will touch those who have them. How pitiful it is for a person to know very well how naked he is before God and to know very well how he participates in unclean sins, and yet attempts to hide and to cover and to reform himself before he will believe in Christ. Such a person can be compared to one who waits till he gets well before he will send for a physician. What a foolish way of thinking and acting! Only when a person honestly acknowledges he is a sinner will he ever be healed.

"Just as I am, . . . I come, I come!" The words of this well-known hymn were written by a sister in the Lord when she was only a little over twenty years of age. From childhood she had had a sense of sin. She often asked herself, How could a person like me ever see God's face? She frequented many churches and met many pastors. She asked them, What shall I do that I may be saved? Many told her, Wait till you are somewhat better and then believe in the Lord Jesus. Some people advised her to pray more and to read the Bible more. Others exhorted her to do more good. This continued on for about seven or eight years; but the result was that she was actually getting worse and not better. Finally, she met an old preacher of the gospel. She asked him this: What must I do that I may be brought close to God and thus be saved? This old man gently laid his hand on her shoulder and replied, "Just as you are, go and meet God." She exclaimed in response, "Do you really think I need not be improved and become better before I can believe in the Lord Jesus?" The old man answered, "Indeed, you need not; you can come just as you are." From that day forward, she began to understand that she could come to the Lord just as she was. And thus did this lady bring her sickness to the Physician sent by God—even Jesus Christ—and she was healed. Not long after returning home, she wrote this hymn: "Just as I am, . . . I come, I come!"

Hence what is grace? Grace is, that just as I am I can come to the Lord. For the Lord Jesus wants sinners to come to Him just as they are.

Now as Jesus answered the Pharisees in this way, they immediately conjured up another question. Disregarding the matter of whether they were sick or well, they charged the Lord and His disciples with being gluttonous people: "The disciples of John fast often, and make supplications; likewise also the disciples of the Pharisees; but thine eat and drink" (Luke 5.33). (Note that fasting here is mentioned in contrast to feasting.) Their words had a double meaning: First, we fast twice a week (see Luke 18.12), but Your disciples eat seven days a week. This is the surface meaning. Second, we are not like Your disciples who both eat and drink. We have good merits in religion; we have done what ordinary people find hard to do. This is not unlike the fact that some people consider being vegetarian to be something virtuous, although the Pharisees esteem themselves as being even more virtuous because they do not eat at all. Whatever good deeds common people cannot do, these Pharisees will do in order to obtain the reputation of being godly.

Since their question had this double meaning, the Lord Jesus answered them separately. He first answered the surface question. "Can ye make the sons of the bride-chamber fast, while the bridegroom is with them? But the days will come, when the bridegroom shall be taken away from them, and then will they fast in those days" (Luke 5.34,35). What Jesus meant was: "I the bridegroom am present, therefore the sons of the bride-chamber do not need to fast." This explains why His disciples do not fast now, since the Lord Jesus has not been taken away. But when He shall be taken away, then His disciples *will* fast. Before the Lord is rejected by men and crucified, the disciples do not need to fast. This answers the question concerning the matter of fasting at its surface level.

But the Lord then used certain parables explaining the incompatibility between the new and the old as His answer to the deeper root question regarding fasting. Why, though, did He use these parables as his mode of reply? It will help us to understand Jesus' use of His parables here if we keep clearly in mind that the Pharisees' mindset was that they had to continually be doing good, that they had to have good deeds in religion and must keep the laws and commandments of God with all their strength in order to please Him. And hence the Lord employed these parables with a view to showing the Pharisees that the things which He brought to the world were totally separate from the rituals and ordinances of the law and that the grace which He brought in was wholly different from the law. The purpose of these parables was therefore to show that law and grace cannot be mixed together. For if they were mixed up, law would no longer be law and grace would no longer be grace. With this understanding, then, let us look into these parables concerning the new and the old which were spoken by the Lord.

Using an Undressed Cloth to Mend an Old Garment

"No man putteth a piece of undressed cloth upon an old garment; for that which should fill it up taketh it from the garment, and a worse rent is made" (Matt. 9.16). Here our Lord shows us the parable of using a piece of undressed cloth to mend an old garment. Such a thing is commonly done, yet the Lord points out its incompatibility. If a piece of undressed cloth is put on an old garment, this new cloth will make a worse rent to the garment. In the Bible, the word garment stands for our righteousness before God. When the garment is torn, the shame of the flesh is exposed. We may think we are well dressed, but there is One who sees us however we are, whether in the dark or in the light. God declares that our garment is torn and that there is no way to cover up our sins and shame. Our past history is so full of uncleanness and sins that we cannot share these things with others. We may keep such matters hidden in our heart, but we cannot hide them from God. And thus the immediate problem is not in proving whether or not this garment is torn, rather it is in proposing what to do to this old and torn garment. Naturally, our own way would be to mend it.

Undressed cloth does not refer to new as opposed to old cloth. It has reference to unshrunken cloth, for the process of manufacturing has not yet been finished. To patch an old garment with such kind of cloth will tear the old garment even more. Spiritually speaking, let it be understood that what many people receive is not the finished work of Christ. They accept the outward name or trademark, but they have not accepted the finished work of Christ on the cross. If they are asked who Jesus Christ is, they will say He is a great moralist, a great religious leader, or a perfect model for us to imitate. Such words are spoken by people who do not believe in the precious blood of our Lord. This is exactly what undressed cloth signifies.

Some people say that Jesus was not born of the virgin Mary, that He is not the Son of God, that His shedding of blood is not for the atoning of sin, that He has not risen from the dead, that His words and deeds before His death serve only as examples to us, and that His death has not too much relationship to us. They consider the works of the Lord Jesus during His thirty-three years of living on earth as enough for them; they have not seen the necessity for the Son of man to be lifted up in death (see John 3.14). They take the death of the Lord Jesus as simply the murder of an ordinary person. They do not see His death as God having died for us. They have never perceived that if the Lord had not died, we all must die. In short, they accept the teachings of the Lord Jesus as "undressed cloth." By cutting a piece out of it, they use it to patch their old and torn garment of unrighteousness.

Even though some may not voice these words, they nonetheless conceive such thought in their heart. Once a brother in the Lord gave a copy of the New Testament to another person. After the latter had read the Four Gospels, he declared that he must learn from Jesus because his conduct was not as perfect as that of Jesus. In doing this, though, he did not acknowledge himself to be a sinner. Such a concept does not prevail only among the heathen; it also can be found among so-called Christians. If you were to ask such a person if his conduct is as good as that of the Lord Jesus, his answer would be an unhesitating no. But if you were to further ask him what he was going to do about it, he woud say that he would give more money to the church and would do more good. Thus, on the one hand, he confesses that his garment is torn, but, on the other hand, he thinks of cutting a piece of undressed cloth and patching up the old garment with it. Yet our Lord states clearly, that if an undressed cloth is used to mend an old garment, it will tear the garment and make the rent worse.

Some people may reason: My garment is torn, I am a sinner before God, therefore I must fast twice a week. Others may ponder: My garment is torn, what shall I do? I know. I will take from my monthly income some money to offer to the church. Or still others may think: I have sinned, what shall I do? I will get up early in the morning to read a chapter of the Bible on my knees. People always conclude that since they have sinned, they must do these or other things to mend their ways. It is like patching up an old garment with piece after piece of undressed cloth. The verdict of the Lord Jesus, however, is that in so doing, a worse rent is made. The more you repair, the worse the rent. You may perhaps speculate that nothing of this sort will ever happen, but the fact is, it *does* happen. For example, someone may be prone to lie. He is determined not to lie again. So, he decides to draw a dark circle on his diary if he lies. The result is that there are more dark circles in his diary than he ever could have imagined. How true it is that the outcome of mending is to cause the rent to be far worse and more evident to everybody. (Please note in this discussion that I am not saying people should not fast, read the Bible, give offerings, and so forth. I am simply explaining how futile it is if we try to use these things as merits to mend our rents and to thus obtain God's favor.)

Using a New Garment to Mend an Old Garment

The picture Luke draws for us is different from those painted by Matthew and Mark. For Luke's account says: "And he spake also a parable unto them: No man rendeth a piece from a new garment and putteth it upon an old garment; else he will rend the new, and also the piece from the new will not agree with the old" (5.36). If a man has two garments, one new and one old, and he cuts a piece from the new garment and puts it on the old, when he sees the old garment is torn, he will be called by everybody a fool. No one would ever do such a thing materially, but odd to say, many always do exactly the same spiritually.

The new cloth which both Matthew and Mark mention is undressed cloth which points to the Lord Jesus before His death—that is to say, before His work is done. When He died and after His work was done, He cried out at His death, "It is finished." His death means the accomplishment of the work of redemption, whereas His life is like an undressed cloth. The cloth Luke writes about in his Gospel is not undressed cloth but finished cloth. If anyone attempts to use the finished cloth of the Lord Jesus to mend his torn garment, he will try to do his best and in addition ask the Lord Jesus to help him where he lacks. Some Christians maintain that we must keep the Ten Commandments. If they are asked whether they have kept them, they will answer that what they cannot do they will ask the Lord Jesus for help. Yet the Lord himself declares that no one rends a piece from a new garment and puts it upon an old torn garment. We cannot do good, therefore it is better to throw away the old altogether and put on the new garment.

We have no way to save ourselves except by confessing our sins. There is no way to get rid of our sins and gain God's favor except to cut off the self-styled good of the flesh—that old rag of ours—and to acknowledge the Lord Jesus Christ as Savior and to trust in His completed work of redemption on the cross. Having been crucified, He has already satisfied the righteous demand of God. The robe which He thus offers to us is new and whole. Nothing needs to be added to it, for on the cross the Lord declares that "it is finished." Many do not know that the work of redemption is already done. They are still thinking that if they are to be saved they must at least do some good; otherwise, how can they be saved? Yet they do not realize that such thought is as foolish as rending a piece of a new garment to put upon an old garment.

The Bible does not tell us to improve ourselves, since the Lord has already done it all. Jesus Christ has borne our sins on the cross; and there He says, "It is finished." He has completed the work and nothing is therefore left to be done. Today we do not need to do anything except to confess that our garment is torn, that we are corrupted and are unable to do any good, and to ask Him to give us a new garment. But if you will to do good, you will have to will it again and again and again. You ought to know that aside from trusting the redemption which the Lord Jesus has accomplished once and for all, there is no other way of salvation.

"No man rendeth a piece from a new garment and putteth it upon an old garment; else he will rend the new, and also the piece from the new will not agree with the old." To rend the new means to destroy the finished work of Jesus Christ. And the new and the old will never agree. For instance, if you take a piece of new, white garment and put it on an old, black garment, the disagreement will instantly be noticeable because of the difference in colors. To mend something it requires a certain compatibility between materials. By putting a piece of a new garment on an old one, the disparity in colors will at once reveal the wear and tear. This is like telling people how unfit things are.

Let us be reminded that the salvation which God gives to us, as represented by a new garment, is totally divergent from our old garment. Are you thinking of filling in what you lack with the Lord Jesus? This is totally unacceptable. If you believe in the Lord Jesus, then you must accept a brand new garment; if you accept only a little of the new garment, you will look even worse. Today we have a new garment which is the righteousness of God. If you wholly accept the Lord, the righteousness of God will cover all your shame and nakedness. But if you contemplate only taking a piece from the new garment—the righteousness of God—and putting it on your old garment, this will only serve to expose your own ugliness.

The teaching of Jesus Christ is but undressed cloth; therefore it cannot save us. It is His finished work of redemption which saves us. Yet we cannot rend a piece from His garment of redemption to put on our ragged conduct. We can only take off completely what we consider our best conduct and put on the new garment of righteousness given by God. For God wants us to throw away our rags and to be clothed with His new garment. What *man* has is a ragged garment; but, thank God, what *He* has is a new garment. Is there any reason for man not to accept this new garment? Hallelujah! The redemption of Jesus Christ is sufficient for every person's salvation. If any man is not saved, it is not because there is no new garment nor because he does not know how to mend his old garment but because he refuses to be clothed with the new garment. On the other hand, a person is saved not because he has good conduct, but because he believes and accepts the finished work of the Lord Jesus. Hence, whether one is saved or not does not depend on his past as a good man or a bad man but depends entirely upon whether he accepts or rejects the redemption of the Lord. All who are willing to receive Jesus Christ shall be saved.

"God so loved the world, that he gave his only begotten Son, that whosoever believeth on him should not perish, but have eternal life" (John 3.16). Hallelujah! This is a fact. Today the Son of God has already died and the new garment is also ready. All you need is to be willing to put it on. Praise the Lord! The problem with salvation is not how valuable is our conduct but how valuable is the cross of Calvary. In this matter of salvation, our conduct has no merit at all; only the death of the Lord Jesus on the cross is meritorious.

The New Wine

"Neither do men put new wine into old wineskins . . ." (Matt. 9.17a). "Garment" points to the external work of the gospel, for it is visible to men. "New wine" refers to the internal work of the gospel because it is invisible to men. The gospel of God includes two aspects: *first*, to make Christ our righteousness, so that we may live before God in this righteousness. Nothing needs to be added because Christ has already become the righteousness of God; it is therefore impossible to add anything to it. Not because our good conduct has pleased God; simply because Christ has died and has been resurrected. Being in Christ, we are looked upon by God as acceptable to Him as is Christ himself. We are saved not because we are different from other people, but because we are in Christ. Being in Christ, we can approach God. Having been clothed with Christ, we can live before God and please Him.

The second aspect of the gospel is for Christ to live in us that we may live before the world. According to the spirit, we live before God; according to the flesh, we live in this world. "Garment" tells of how God gives us Christ and has made Him to be our righteousness so that we may live *before God.* "Wine" speaks of how God gives us Christ and has made Him to be our life and power that we may accept His control and by Him live *before men.*

Some people complain in the following manner: Indeed, I am saved and have received forgiveness of sins before God; but my daily life is still the same as before. What can I do about it? Please remember that God has not only clothed you outwardly with a new garment in order to cover and adorn you, He has also put inside you a power like that of the new wine which will dissolve all the old things. We should know that salvation has this double aspect: that of the *objective* which is before God, and that of the *subjective* which is within us. In other words, there is justification on the one hand and regeneration on the other.

It is absolutely impossible to be regenerated and not be justified, or justified without being regenerated. Justification obtains for us a new position before God, whereas regeneration gives us a new life in us. Some people pay attention only to justification without so much as considering this aspect of regeneration; yet other people over-emphasize regeneration and overlook justification. Because of their misconception none of these people realizes that regeneration and justification happen at the same time, and thus they can hold such prejudiced views. Actually justification and regeneration balance each other well.

In the third chapter of the Gospel according to John, the word "must" occurs a number of times. We will focus on two of them. In verse 7 we find, "Ye *must* be born anew"; and in verse 14 it reads, "Even so *must* the Son of man be lifted up." The same word in Greek is used in both cases. What is said in verse 14 is objective, for the Lord Jesus is lifted up that we may receive the forgiveness of sins and be justified. What is stated in verse 7 is subjective, because this will give us new life. Being justified, we have liberty before God; having been regenerated, we have a new life within us.

Some people may speculate within themselves as follows: "I am very much afraid to approach God because I do not know if He will save or not. Will God say to me, 'Depart from me, you wicked one!'? I am a sinner, I do not know whether God wants me or not." To such people we would say: Do not be afraid, for the Lord Jesus has already come and has died for our sins. He has already satisfied God's justice, and He has also been resurrected. Today all who come to

God through the Lord Jesus Christ shall be saved. The Lord himself has assured us that "he that believeth on him is not judged" (John 3.18a). Paul also declared that "by him every one that believeth is justified from all things, from which ye could not be justified by the law of Moses" (Acts 13.39). You who trust in the Lord today are justified. You ought to know that through Him you can come before God with a conscience void of fear because "there is . . . now no condemnation to them that are in Christ Jesus" (Rom. 8.1).

You know you are saved; nevertheless you feel miserable, because to will is present with you but to do that which is good is not in you (see Rom. 7.18). You have seen changes in the lives of other believers, yet in yourself you see no change. You are saved as much as they are; why then are there changes in them but none in you? Why is your living not much different from what you were before? You cry over your defeats and weaknesses. You ponder over the matter of your salvation. You have to acknowledge that you are saved and that you have eternal life; but being the kind of person as you are, you ask yourself if you are really saved. You can hardly believe so. Therefore, you try harder to do good, to pray, and to read the Bible more, and to discipline yourself more strictly in order to please God. You seem to see some results in three or five days, yet the effect is all in vain when measured by months or years. This is exactly what the Lord Jesus meant when He said we must not mend the old garment with a piece from the new garment; that after being saved, we ought to use the new wine—the power of this new life—to overcome all outward entanglements. The new wine is put within us to give us new life and the power of living.

All who are justified are regenerated. Whoever has the new garment has also the new wine. Hallelujah! God has already put this regenerated life in us; henceforth we are new men. The new wine is the power of the gospel. We have this power in us, causing us to live a victorious life. The question now is, Where is the new wine to be put?

The New Wine-skins and the Old Wine-skins

"Neither do men put new wine into old wine-skins: . . . but they put new wine into fresh wine-skins . . ." Why should the new wine not be put into old wine-skins (according to Jewish custom, wine is put into skins)? Because the new wine has tremendous power of expansion. It will burst the old wine-skin if it is put into it, and then the wine will be spilled.

What is the meaning of the old wine-skins? Some people say that the old wine-skins represent us. This kind of interpretation is not correct. Since the old garment does not stand for us, how can the old wine-skins represent us? We ought to consider the context of these words. As the old garment points to the so-called righteousness of us men, so the old wine-skins refers to our natural good conduct. This old wine-skin is related to fasting in the preceding passage. Fasting enables us to boast that we are not like the tax-collector since we fast twice a week. What causes us to boast before God is the old wine-skins.

Hence old wine-skins speaks of both the better conduct we consider ourselves as having had before we were saved as well as the good works which we may depend on after we are saved. We Christians may turn back like the Galatian believers and think of pleasing God by keeping the law. We try to rely on our own strength to obtain His favor. This is what Paul observed in the third chapter of Galatians: "Having begun in the spirit, are ye now perfected in the flesh?" (v.3) All who begin with the Lord Jesus and then try to be perfected by themselves are putting new wine into old wine-skins.

In days past on up to present days, no one has been able to mix Christianity and Judaism together and still preserve both. For the result of such a mixture can only cause Christianity to be unlike Christianity and Judaism to be unlike Judaism. Both will lose their original flavor. God will not tolerate such a thing. The Roman church has combined Judaism with Christianity. On the one hand they adopt the customs and rituals of the Old Covenant; on the other hand they embrace the name of the New Covenant. Is this Christianity? No. Is this Judaism? The answer is equally no. Add Judaism to Christianity and the result is neither Judaism nor Christianity.

The new wine can only be put into fresh wine-skins. Only thus can it be powerful and effective. The new wine must follow the principle of the New Covenant and then it will please God. Having this new wine in you, you have a power within that can control you. If you are not saved, you will not have such an experience, and neither will you change. But if you are saved, you will invariably sense within you a law which is in control of you.

There was a mother who was very careful in speech, but she had a son who was most talkative. Each time they went to visit their relatives, the mother would tell the son that whenever he spoke too much, she would pull his sleeves as a sign that he should close his mouth and speak no more. But during the conversation, her son would talk incessantly and completely ignore the mother's pulling of his sleeve. How marvelous it is for a Christian that when he goes out alone with no one at his side and becomes too talkative, he feels within him a Person pulling him, saying, That is enough. For if he continues to speak, he will be ungodly and unlike a Christian. As soon as he listens to the inner voice and stops speaking, he experiences peace. What is this? This is the new wine.

Can we put the new wine into the old wine-skins? No. It is right to inscribe the words of the Bible upon our heart, but to write them on the wall is like putting them into old wine-skins. In other words, this is trying to keep the law by our own effort. The law of the Old Covenant is external, while that of the New Covenant is internal. Here is the difference between the New Covenant and the Old. Just as the people under the Old Covenant could not in themselves keep the Ten Commandments, even so the Christians under the New Covenant cannot keep such external commandments either. The Old Covenant is inscribed on stone tablets, the words of which we in ourselves have no power to keep; but the New Covenant is written upon the heart, thus giving us strength to keep it. Thank God, we have no need for words written on paper to remind us. We instead have One who reminds us from within.

The new wine cannot be put into old wine-skins. The new wine must be put into fresh wine-skins. God has not commanded us to keep the outward law, but He does command us to keep the inward law. For the law within us is living and not dead. Romans 8 speaks of "the law of the Spirit of life." This law is in us and it enables us to keep the law of God. Oh, we have not only the new garment outside but the new wine inside as well. We have not only righteousness but also new life. The new wine is put into the fresh wine-skins that we may live in newness of life.

The Old Wine

"And no man having drunk old wine desireth new; for he saith, The old is good" (Luke 5.39). This is the consensus of the world. All who have drunk the old wine will not desire the new. Yet, God will not give old wine to man to drink. The Jews rejected what the Lord Jesus gave to them because they had drunk too much of the old wine. How our minds, too, are drunk with old wine. We think that it will be well if we do good and improve ourselves. In actual fact, however, if a person drinks only the old wine, there is no new power—no real explosive power—in him. If he does not drink the new wine, he will be powerless year after year. He who thinks of pleasing God with his own good conduct is following a futile path. Only by trusting in the Lord Jesus Christ and drinking the new wine can a person please God.

Having studied these parables of the new and the old, we can now clearly understand that there is absolutely no way to mix up law and grace. Let us never for a moment try to *mend* our rags with the righteousness of Christ; simply *put on* Christ. Let us never think that we have to do good after we are saved; let us simply trust Christ as our life and let Him live himself out through us.

2 Gleanings from the Parable of the Prodigal Son

Scripture Reading: Luke 15.11–32

I have spoken on this passage a number of times. My burden today is not to go over the entire parable, but only to focus attention on several points for our consideration. They are fragmentary.

One

"But when he came to himself he said, How many hired servants of my father's have bread enough and to spare, and I perish here with hunger! I will arise and go to my father, and will say unto him, Father, I have sinned against heaven, and in thy sight: I am no more worthy to be called thy son; make me as one of thy hired servants" (vv.17–19). A sinner who is pressed into awakening by environment always embraces a particular conception towards his salvation.

He will think about how he can be saved. He will ask himself, What is the condition for my salvation?

If you were to ask sinners how they can be saved, you would receive from them various ways of salvation. God has His way of salvation, and sinners have their ways. A hundred sinners have a hundred different ways of salvation, based on their own concepts and evaluations. So, too, this prodigal son had his particular concept about salvation. He thought when he would see his father that undoubtedly his father would severely scold him. And thus the prodigal would probably prepare himself to answer as follows: "I have wasted away all my inheritance; I have no right, Father, to use any of your money; but you are a rich man who hires many servants; would you therefore simply hire me as you hire other people?" Without question, his concept of salvation is not to be a son, but to become a hired servant!

The salvation of God which a sinner conceives of is always: I give You work, and You give me wages. According to the measure of how much I work for You, You give me certain wages—yet not as a son, but as a hired servant.

Two

"And he rose, and came to his father. But while he was yet afar off, his father saw him, and was moved with compassion, and ran, and fell on his neck, and *kissed* him. And the son said unto him, Father, I have sinned against heaven, and in thy sight: I am no more worthy to be called thy son. *But* the father said to his servants, Bring forth quickly the best robe, and put it on him; and put a ring on his hand, and shoes on his feet" (vv.20–22). This prodigal son arose and went back to his father. When he saw his father, he spoke to him the words which he had premeditated. But after he came to the point of saying, "I am no more worthy to be called thy son," he was interrupted from finishing his speech. *But* the father ordered . . .! Hallelujah! I thank God, because salvation is according to His thought, not according to mine. If salvation were to have been in accordance with the thought of the prodigal son, it would have resulted only in his becoming a hired servant. How man's thought is full of law—that is to say, man can only expect to get what he has worked for.

This prodigal had prepared a speech for his father, but he was so touched by the father's love that he could not finish his speech with the words, "Make me as one of thy hired servants." By carefully reading the context we find that he was given no chance to say so by his father. The latter had heard enough. Without waiting for his son to finish his speech, he ordered his servants to bring out quickly the best robe to put on his son, the ring to be put on his hand, and shoes to be put on his feet.

Such salvation as this reveals how God will treat you and me: it is not how we think we will be treated by Him. If it were according to *our* thinking, we would at best be a hired servant forever. We think of ourselves as sinners, but God declares we are children. We think we will perish, but He seats us at the table. There is absolutely no danger of saying too much about the grace of God. We think we are not worthy to be called sons, but He does exceedingly above that which we could ever think of. Let us thank God, for salvation is not according to our thinking and concept, but according to His.

When the prodigal son was still afar off, the father saw him and was moved with compassion. A certain man fell among robbers, but a certain Samaritan saw him and was moved with compassion (see Luke 10.33). What is compassion? Compassion is exhibited towards one who has fallen to a low position. Compassion is always shown from above, expressed towards a pitiful situation. Suppose the son had come back with abundance; the father would have had no way to show compassion. How was he moved with compassion? Only when he saw his own son fallen to the position of a beggar. Hence a beggar was accepted back as a son; one who had begged at the door was now made to sit at the table. We as beggars, far away from God, move the compassion of God towards us.

Let us notice another thing here; the prodigal thought he was no longer worthy to be called a son, and therefore only wished to be a hired servant; *but* the father ordered to have put on him the best robe, a ring, and shoes. This expresses the *riches* of *God* and not our own poverty. For salvation speaks of the exceeding riches of God. How often we think how unworthy we are. Even when we are somewhat awakened, we still are uncertain whether God will forgive us if we pray. It seems to us that people such as we are, are hopeless in prayer. But may I tell you, you are wrong! A man who is rich beyond computation thinks not of how much his son has spent, but how much he can give to his son.

Here is an inadequate illustration. Once I met a rich man's son whom I exhorted with earnestness to repent and believe in the Lord. One day he brought me to see his father. I asked the father not to hinder his son from believing the Lord and told him that once his son would be saved, he would never waste his father's money. But the father said that what he had was money—a great deal of it, and he was not at all afraid of his son spending it. Likewise, our God is not afraid of our spending. We may think He has only a hundred dollars, but we want to spend a hundred and one dollars. We may be afraid that after we have spent all of it, we would have nothing more to spend. But what our Father has is riches, therefore we should not limit God. Remember that salvation represents the wealth of God with supplies which are inexhaustible.

You may reflect that you have a sin which you cannot ever overcome. But let me ask you, Can you say God can do nothing about that sin of yours? Many times we Christians are weak and prone to sin, and our conscience tells us we are finished. But what the conscience tells us is our own condition. Conscience tells us what we are, whereas the precious blood tells us how God treats us. And our conscience is sprinkled with the blood. So, what we now have is not merely a conscience and some blood in a basin, but a conscience sprinkled with the blood. Do not separate the conscience from the blood nor the blood from the conscience. It is a conscience sprinkled with the blood, and therefore it is whiter than snow.

God has a robe for you to be clothed with and He is not afraid of your selling it; He has a ring for you to wear, and is not afraid of your pawning it; shoes for you to put on, and is not afraid of your wearing them out. Children of God should be beautifully adorned. Those in the house of God are bountifully supplied.

Three

"And bring the fatted calf, and kill it, and let us eat, and make merry" (v.23). The robe, the ring and the shoes were for the son to enjoy personally, for all these could only be put on one person. However, the fatted calf was not merely for a single person to consume, but rather it says this: "Let *us* eat, and make merry." Let me give you a new thought today, which is the *joy of God.* On the night I was saved, the more I thought about it the merrier I became and the more I sang. I did not mind if there were neither rhyme nor tune. And such is the joy of being saved. Nevertheless, this Scripture verse tells us that it was the father who was joyful. It is therefore the joy of God in His saving a soul that is being expressed here. We usually think when a sinner is saved, how glad *he* is, and how glad *we* are. We fail to realize how joyful God the Father also is when He saves a sinner. If we see this, we can begin to understand the Father's heart.

Four

"But he [the elder son] answered and said to the father, Lo, these many years do I serve thee, and I never transgressed a commandment of thine; and yet thou never gavest me a kid, that I might make merry *with my friends*" (v.29). These were the words of the elder son to his father. The heart of the elder son was in the father giving *him* happiness, but the younger son who spent everything and yet returned home gave joy to his father. The elder son was indeed dutiful in the father's house, yet his fault lay in only desiring the father to give him joy. The father wanted him to come in and rejoice with the father. From this we ought to understand God's heart that He wants us to be merry with Him. The elder son, however, wanted a kid with which to enjoy himself with his own friends. Keep in mind that God in His ways never gives anything to anyone just for that one to enjoy: He always wants men to enjoy together with Him.

Five

Let us next compare these two things: "kiss" and "table." The father fell on the prodigal's neck and kissed him. Such kissing made the son's heart glad and satisfied. By the father's kissing him, he knew his father had forgiven him and would not remember his iniquity any more. Thus he received the freedom and satisfaction of sins forgiven. The son now sat at the table, and this gave joy and satisfaction to the father's heart because he had today got his son back. Many do not know how glad God is to have people saved. They may speculate they are saved because they pleaded hard. Who really knows how glad God is in saving souls! Let it be known that in saving souls, God gets great pleasure.

When we hear the Father say, "I have forgiven your sins," we have peace and joy. We need not seek for any further proof. A word from God is sufficient. When He says He forgives, we are forgiven. Yet how pitiful it is if we only have part of the joy and do not fully enter into God's joy, which is, to enjoy the joy of God as well as to give joy to Him. Worship comes out of joy in the Lord. Worship is more than thanksgiving, it is a rejoicing in God. We take His joy as our joy. The psalmist says, "unto God my exceeding joy" (Ps. 43.4). May we all make God our exceeding great joy.

Six

"For this my son was dead, and is alive again; he was *lost* and is *found*. And they began to be merry" (v.24). God says let us be merry for two reasons: one is, this son was dead and is alive again; and two, this son was lost and is found. "Dead, and is alive again" is what the son gets personally. "Lost, and is found" is what the father gets. Formerly he was a fallen son, now he comes to be son again. Men were originally created by God, but they fell as though dead. The Lord Jesus came to save men and cause them to be raised from the dead. This is resurrection. But our emphasis today is on "*lost* and is *found*."

In Luke 15, there are three parables: that of the

lost sheep, of the lost silver, and of the lost son. Have you ever thought of *who* lost them? We usually focus on how pitiful the lost sheep is. It may wander among rugged stones and along thorny paths. Yet we lose sight of the shepherd who loses his sheep. It is also the shepherd who suffers loss. How pitiful he is. We likewise focus on the lost piece of silver. We wonder where it fell. But we forget that it is the woman who loses the silver. She is the one who incurs loss. And in this last parable, we reckon how miserable must be the prodigal—he being in a far country and not even having the husks of grain to assuage his hunger. We rejoice for him as he returns home because great is his blessing. But who is the one who has lost a son? Certainly not the son, only the father. It is the father who suffers. It is the father who has spent so much on the son's education—and for nothing. Hence, the father says, this son was lost and is found. Therefore the father and the others begin to be merry.

Have we ever thought of how each return and each obedience gives joy to the Father's heart? The peak of the gospel lies not in what the sinner receives but what God receives. You and I waste the money, and God incurs the loss. How we should give ourselves wholly to Him. How much can we give to God? Let us not assume it does not matter if we grow a little bit cold. We should know what loss our little bit of coldness gives to God. Let us not rationalize that it is only a small thing to love the world and be mixed up with it. We ought to realize that this has much to do with our relationship to God: how this will cause much loss to the Father. Each time we come to ourselves as did the prodigal, we rededicate ourselves to Him. Each time we are willing to lay down ourselves that God may gain, we give Him something to be joyful about.

My personal gain or loss is nothing; what really counts is that God should gain. Every time I reflect on the fact that I gladden the heart of the Father by choosing the way of obedience, how good it is. God can create the universe and He can add many things to men, but He has the possibility of losing men's hearts. He never coerces anybody. When I consider the greatness, the omnipotence, and the all-sufficiency of God who is the Creator of all things, I marvel that He could gain anything from a tiny worm or a speck of dust that I myself am. Yet He says, "Let *us* make merry"! The return of the prodigal son made God glad. The God who fills the universe rejoices at our little obedience. Consecration is not forced on us to put us down; rather, it enables us to enter the joy of God, that he may rejoice because of us. How wonderful this is! May we enter into the Father's joy today, and give God cause to be glad!

3 The Better Blood

And Cain told Abel his brother. And it came to pass, when they were in the field, that Cain rose up against Abel his brother, and slew him. And Jehovah said unto Cain, Where is Abel thy brother? And he said, I know not: am I my brother's keeper? And he said, What hast thou done? the voice of thy brother's blood crieth unto me from the ground. And now cursed art thou from the ground, which hath opened its mouth to receive thy brother's blood from thy hand. (Gen. 4.8–11)

And to Jesus the mediator of a new covenant, and to the blood of sprinkling that speaketh better than that of Abel. (Heb. 12.24)

This is he that came by water and blood, even Jesus Christ; not with the water only, but with the water and with the blood. . . . For there are three who bear witness, the Spirit, and the water, and the blood; and the three agree in one. (1 John 5.6,8)

These passages of Scripture speak of the blood of

our Lord as well as the blood of Abel. And the blood of our Lord speaks better than that of Abel. Why is it better? Let us look into this matter.

One

Why was Abel killed? Because Cain was jealous of him. For God looked favorably on Abel and his sacrifice but not on Cain and his offering. Consequently, Cain became jealous and killed his brother one day in the field.

Why did the Jews bring the Lord Jesus Christ to the Roman governor? From the record we learn this: "he [Pilate] knew that for envy they had delivered him up" (Matt. 27.18). The Jews killed the Lord Jesus because of their jealousy of him.

Abel was envied by Cain, and hence he was killed by Cain. Likewise, the Lord Jesus was envied by the Jews, and so He was killed by them.

Two

Why does the blood of the Lord Jesus speak better than that of Cain? The blood of Abel cried from the ground, asking God to avenge according to *justice* the sin of shedding his blood. But the blood of the Lord Jesus cries to God to deal with men according to *grace* and to forgive their sin of shedding His blood. The blood of Abel asked for the execution of God's justice, and once this justice was carried out, the son of Adam—the sinful Cain—had no place to hide. The blood of the Lord Jesus also, in a sense, demands justice, yet when God administers His justice, He "forgives us our sins, and cleanses us from all unrighteousness" (1 John 1.9)—for the Lord Jesus died for us. God cannot punish us again since He has already punished Christ. God asked Cain, "Where is Abel thy brother?" Cain answered, "I know not: am I my brother's keeper?" If God should ask us today, "Where is Jesus thy brother?", we praise and thank God, for we may reply: "He was indeed killed by us, but His blood does not accuse us." Hallelujah, the blood of the Lord Jesus does not accuse us! This is a marvelous salvation.

Three

Why does the Scripture say that the blood speaks? This is parallel to what 1 John says that the blood bears witness. The blood has a double function before God: one, that it propitiates for our sins; and the other, that it guarantees for us. Many only see how the blood of the Lord Jesus propitiates for their sins before God, they do not see how His blood also serves as their *security* before him. His blood propitiates for our sins on earth, and it bears witness for us in heaven, testifying to the accomplished work of redemption. So that the Lord Jesus shed His blood on earth to be our Savior and now He is in heaven as our *eternal* Savior.

What, among the Jews, always took place on the great day of atonement as recorded in Leviticus 16? On the one hand, the blood flowed from the altar to the ground; and on the other hand, it was carried by the high priest into the holiest of all to be sprinkled upon the ark of the covenant.The blood which flowed to the ground would dry up in a few days, but that which was brought into the holiest of all would speak forever for us. The blood that flowed to the ground was for atonement, whereas the blood carried into the holiest of all spoke before Jehovah and bore witness for the Jews. Hence our Lord has His blood shed on the one hand for the sake of propitiating for and forgiving us of our sins, and on the other hand to speak and bear witness for us before God. The blood sprinkled in heaven bears continuing witness to the fact of the blood having propitiated for our sins on earth.

So what does the blood bear witness to? The blood before God represents the fact of propitiation before Him. It quietly bears witness before Him, guaranteeing our eternal peace. Had the blood not been shed on earth, would there ever have been the blood sprinkled before God? The blood bears witness for *God,* it saying that God loves us; otherwise, where would this blood have come from? At the same time, it bears witness for *us*, it declaring that we are saved; else why should the blood be shed at all? The blood therefore testifies to the love of God as well as to our salvation. Furthermore, it also testifies against Satan so that he can accuse us no more. Praise and thank God, the blood of the Lord Jesus speaks better than that of Abel, because this blood is not for vengeance but for peace.

Once our Lord Jesus shed his blood, the work was forever done. Today we have the assurance of salvation before God. Someone says he is saved because once upon a time he repented; another says he is saved because he felt so good after prayer on a certain occasion. But such explanations are undependable. It is because of the blood of the Lord which bears continued witness before God that anyone is a saved person. For His blood speaks better than that of Abel. *Abel's* blood cried from the earth, saying, I want the blood of him who shed mine. *Jesus'* blood speaks from heaven, saying, I forgive those who killed me. The blood of our Lord forever bears witness for us in heaven. Let us all who are saved therefore praise and thank God because Jesus' blood is testifying today in heaven.

How little we understand how the blood of our Lord Jesus speaks! If we truly know, we will perceive fresh meaning as we contemplate His blood. Praise God, the blood of Christ not only washes all our sins away but at the same time it bears witness for us before God. In the face of such a witness, He can never cast us away. Christ has died and been raised from among the dead. Who then can accuse us? We do praise and thank our God.

4 Sin and the Body

> Knowing this, that our old man was crucified with him, that the body of sin might be done away, that so we should no longer be in bondage to sin. (Rom. 6.6)
>
> Even so reckon ye also yourselves to be dead unto sin, but alive unto God in Christ Jesus. Let not sin therefore reign in your mortal body, that ye should obey the lusts thereof; neither present your members unto sin as instruments of unrighteousness; but present yourselves unto God, as alive from the dead, and your members as instruments of righteousness unto God. For sin shall not have dominion over you: for ye are not under law, but under grace. (Rom. 6.11-14)

These two passages in Romans present to us clearly the relationship between sin and the body. Let us discuss them together briefly.

One

"Knowing this, that our old man was crucified with him, that the body of sin might be done away, that so we should no longer be in bondage to sin" (Rom. 6.6). Before we were born again and received the new man, all we had was the old man, though we definitely did not deem ourselves to be such. It is only after we have the new man that our old man begins to be exposed. This old man includes all that we inherited from the old creation. In being crucified the Lord Jesus not only dies for our sins but also takes the sinful human race with Him to the cross. His death is the death of mankind, for in His incarnation He has joined himself with humanity. His death is also the death of our old man, because by faith we are joined to Him. The statement that "our old man was crucified with him" is an accomplished fact which is done for us by the Lord Jesus.

What is the purpose of our being so crucified with Him? "That the body of sin might be done away, that so we should no longer be in bondage to sin." Here do we see the relationship between sin and the body. The reason we are in bondage to sin is because this body of sin has not been done away. The painful influence of sin lies in this body. Its stronghold and territory are in this body. We are in bondage to sin because the body is in bondage to sin. Unless the body is dealt with by the cross, the entire person will be under the bondage of sin.

Other passages of Scripture also connect sin and the body, for the body is the dwelling place of sin:

"But sin which dwelleth in me. . . . in me, that is, in my flesh" (Rom. 7.17,18); "with the flesh the law of sin" (v.25b); "Put to death therefore your members which are upon the earth: fornication, uncleanness, passion, evil desire, and covetousness" (Col. 3.5).

In the eyes of God, the human body is truly "the body of sin" because sin is the master of the body. From the above Scripture verses, we cannot fail to see how tightly knit together sin and the body are. All the sins we ever commit are affected by the body. It is not difficult to understand the reason why: "lust, when it hath conceived, beareth sin" (James 1.15a). The root of sin is in lust, and lust waits in ambush in the body: "the flesh with the passions and the lusts thereof" (Gal. 5.24b). As a matter of fact, many sins are committed due to physiological reasons. Because there are lusts in the body, therefore such sins are produced.

For this reason, if anyone desires to be delivered from the power of sin and not to be in bondage to it, he must overcome his body. In Romans 6.6 the apostle tells us how our Lord delivers us from the tyranny of the body. The Lord Jesus took our old man to the cross with Him, so as to do away with this our body of sin. "Done away" (or "destroyed") in the original Greek means "to render idle, inactive, inoperative, to cause to cease." By what He has accomplished on the cross, the Lord Jesus renders our body of sin inoperative and inactive so that we are no longer in bondage to sin. The body still exists; it is not destroyed in the sense of being annihilated. It simply finds that its lusts which are due to its physiological structure are disabled and withered by the Lord. Each one of us has his or her natural weakness, but we all may overcome through the cross.

Two

"Even so reckon ye also yourselves to be dead unto sin" (v.11). Verse 6 tells us three things: a fact, a purpose, and a result. Co-death is a fact, "done away" is the purpose of co-death, and overcoming sin is the final result. Now verse 11 shows us how to put verse 6 into practice. The way is to reckon what the Lord Jesus has done as fact. Verse 6 states we were dead with Christ and the body of sin was rendered inoperative. Now, we believe all this to be true. We accept the work of Christ in having dealt with our body on the cross. Soon we shall see all the passions and lusts, natural inclinations and delights of the flesh being put to death by the Holy Spirit.

Three

"Let not sin therefore reign in your mortal body, that ye should obey the lusts thereof" (v.12). Since the salvation of the Lord Jesus is perfect, in that He already *has crucified* our old man, *"therefore"* we now may be freed. If sin should reign in our mortal body, it is not because we *must* obey it, but rather because we *want* sin to reign over us. So the question before us is this—What would our will choose? The question of whether or not the sins of the body can be overcome is already solved, simply because the Lord Jesus has already had our old man crucified. But, what do we now choose? If we choose to "let not sin" reign in our mortal body, the lusts of the flesh cannot force us to obey them. Yet if we do not exercise our will to choose that which the Lord has accomplished for us, and even though the Lord has already crucified the old man, we in our experience shall still be in bondage to sin.

Many believers do not understand why they do not see the effectiveness of co-death in their lives after they have believed in the teaching of co-death. Probably quite a few are stuck right here. For though they have *believed* in the truthfulness of the fact found in verse 6, nevertheless the accomplished fact of our Lord will not be in effect unless their *will* decides to "let not sin" reign over them. For if their will still *desires* after sin, their believing will be useless. The body is firmly joined to sin—it as a matter of fact is called "the body of sin"; however, a believer is able to "let not sin" reign in the body because of the salvation of the Lord. Though lusts still dwell in the flesh, believers are nonetheless under no obligation to them.

Four

"Neither present your members unto sin as instruments of unrighteousness; but present yourselves unto God, as alive from the dead, and your members as instruments of righteousness unto God" (v.13). This is the second time the idea of "not" is mentioned. The first one in verse 12 ("let not") relates to the body; the second one, here in verse 13 ("neither"), concerns the members. The first one points to the entire body; the second refers to the parts. The first one is to not let sin reign in the mortal body; the second is to not let sin control any member of the body.

How intimately connected are our sin, the entire human body, and the members of the body. Sin needs the body to be its dwelling place, and it also needs the members to be its instruments. Without the body and its members, sin has no way to express itself. For believers to overcome the sin of the body, they must not let sin reign; to overcome the sins of the members, they must not let their members be instruments of sin.

Following this comes the matter of the two "presentings" (or consecrations). One is to present "yourselves" and the other is to present "your members." The two "nots" spoken of above are negative in character; the two "presents" are positive. To present the self is to present the entire body, by exercising one's will to consecrate himself wholly to God that He may be the Lord of all. To present the members is to consecrate member by member to God to be instruments of righteousness. All these consecrations must be done in the realm of resurrection. For a believer to overcome all the natural passions, lusts and inclinations of his body as well as the weaknesses, uncleannesses and sins due to the physiological realm, he must—on the basis of his faith in co-death with Christ—exercise his will to deny sin its influence in the body and its power to express itself through the members. Moreover, on the basis of the Lord's resurrection he must offer himself to God and actively practice righteousness with his members.

Now if a Christian believes in co-death and yet he

does not exercise his will to resist sin, his faith is dead and ineffectual. Likewise, if he merely wills to resist, and yet he does not will on the basis of co-death with Christ, his will is totally in vain. Hence by negatively not letting sin reign and positively believing in his co-death and co-resurrection with Christ, the believer can present himself and his members to God.

Five

Such positive consecration is an important step in overcoming the body. Our will must yield to God. Otherwise victory is impossible. We must not only will not to sin but also will to have God. Not only will not to sin, but also will to practice righteousness. Positively advance as well as negatively retreat. If we present ourselves and our members to God with simpleness of heart according to His order, the God who calls us will accept our consecration and fill us with himself so that we may do His will in all things. Such consecration needs to be constantly renewed. We believe the resurrection life of Christ will thus be lived out from within us. And the result is: "sin shall not have dominion over you" (v.14a).

5 The Meaning of Baptism

And now why tarriest thou? arise, and be baptized, and wash away thy sins, calling on his name. (Act 22.16)

Or are ye ignorant that all we who were baptized into Christ Jesus were baptized into his death? We were buried therefore with him through baptism into death: that like as Christ was raised from the dead through the glory of the Father, so we also might walk in newness of life. (Rom. 6.3,4)

What Baptism Means

What is the meaning of baptism? What is the teaching of the Bible concerning baptism? What is the emphasis? Why does the word of God command us to be baptized? Before answering these questions, let us first ask why we usually wash ourselves in water? It is because of the fear of physical uncleanness. Dust and dirt may be on our body, so we wash them away. No one will go to the water to wash in order to make himself unclean. People wash in water to get clean; otherwise they will not go into water. Hence, the Bible teaches that the first meaning of baptism is to wash oneself clean. If it were not for cleansing, we would not be baptized.

We should also ask why we throw things into the water. Why do you cast the garbage into the water? Because you want to get rid of it. And the Bible makes clear that the second meaning of baptism is to be buried. You do not want it anymore, therefore you bury it.

Wash Away Sins

In the passage we have quoted from the book of Acts, it records how Ananias was sent by the Holy Spirit with a clear vision and with the word of God to Saul: "And now why tarriest thou? arise, and be baptized, and wash away thy sins, calling on his name." So then, why be baptized? The purpose is clearly to wash away one's sins.

However, this Scripture verse can easily be misunderstood. Sometime ago two brothers came from the north of the River Yangtze and asked me about washing away sins. Suppose a person is not baptized, they asked; are his sins unwashed? Many other people have the same misapprehension. The Bible plainly says, Wash away your sins. What does it mean?

Furthermore, the Bible not only denies that baptism is merely a ritual, it also reveals to us that baptism is a testimony. Why do people go into the water?

That they may testify before God and men and angels and Satan that they have believed in Jesus and that what Christ has accomplished is true, perfect and trustworthy. This is what baptism expresses and testifies.

Ananias called Saul to rise up and be baptized. Why? For the sake of washing away his sins. Yet Ananias did not suggest that baptism could get rid of sins, for it is not water baptism itself that washes away sins but it is the reality which baptism expresses and testifies to that washes away sins. The water of the whole earth cannot wash away one single sin, yet what the water of baptism represents and testifies to—even the blood of the Lord Jesus—*is* able to wash away *all* sins. Have you believed? If you have, arise and be baptized to wash away your sins.

It ought to be clearly realized that none who in God's eyes is unclean and whose sins are unforgiven may be baptized. No one who is ignorant of his sins being forgiven and of his having eternal life can be baptized. It is not right for such a one to be baptized. Every one who goes into the baptismal waters is to testify to what he knows. What is testimony? To testify is to bear witness to what is seen and known. First seeing, then testifying. He who has not seen cannot testify. For this reason, one must know his sins forgiven through the washing by the blood of the Lord before he can testify of this reality before men.

Such being the case, infant baptism is improper. If the baptized one is not able to testify, his baptism is void. The baptism of a person who is baptized in unbelief or before believing in the Lord Jesus does not count. Only the one who can testify to the fact that his sins are forgiven is qualified to be baptized. For what he does in the water bears witness to what Christ has accomplished.

What should one do after he knows he is saved and his sins are forgiven? He should testify. How? Where? The first testimony is given in the water of baptism. For this testimony is made before God and men and angels and Satan to the effect that his sins are forgiven, they are washed away. This is therefore the first meaning of baptism as well as its condition.

The Two Sides of Sin

Whatever the Bible teaches is most amazing. Sin has its two sides just as the way God deals with man's sin is also two-sided. One side of sin is towards God, and the other side of sin is in us. The sin before God needs to be forgiven and washed by Him, while the sin within us must be overcome and delivered. As regards the sin before God, the Lord Jesus has borne our sins; as regards the sin within us, we must reckon ourselves as dead to it. For the sin before God, there is the washing of the *blood* of the Lord; for the sin in us, there is the deliverance of the *cross* of the Lord. The sin before God requires God's forbearance and forgiveness; the sin in us demands liberty and emancipation.

We will not go into the nature of these two sides of sin at this time, but we will focus on the effects of these two sides of sin. First, then, the sin before God.

Such sin will cause you to lose peace in your heart. As you think of judgment, hell, death, and the end of human life, you know you have sinned before God. When you reflect on the holiness, righteousness and the determinate will of God, you tremble in fear. All who have not believed in the Lord Jesus as Savior will have such experience. If you do not, I pity you because you are so insensitive and ignorant of your danger. All who ponder a little on hell, death, eternity, judgment and sin will doubtless have no peace and they are fearful even of thinking about punishment, death and the final end.

Yet man has sin in him as well as sin before God. Once a seminary student told his professor that he found a new thing in the Bible, even the truth of sin. The professor responded this way: "Why, you have just found the truth of sin in the Bible today? I had already found it in my own heart!" One does not need to discover the reality of sin in the Bible, he can find it in his heart. Everybody can prove that sin is not only before God but is also within him.

Suppose you frequently lose your temper. You rationalize that outside things stir you up. Actually, it is not any outside thing, it is a fire within you which often breaks out. You try to suppress it but you cannot. As opportunity arises, it explodes. When an explosive explodes, it cannot blame an outside fire; it has the explosive material within. Sin comes out of the heart. Many theorize that their mind being unclean and full of sins is the result of their being tempted by the pornography they read. But may I ask you if your heart is wholly pure when you are under the purest environment?

Sin dwells in man and is deeply rooted. Many sinners love to gamble and smoke opium not because they are drawn by outside things but because they are compelled by the sin resident within them. Sin will receive its punishment before God, but the sin within has power over you to force you to do things you do not want to do. You may exercise your will power to suppress it for a while, but as soon as it has opportunity it will explode forth. This is the actual situation of man: sin reigns within: it has power to impel us to do what we would not want to do, because we are its slaves.

The Two Sides of Deliverance

Just as sin has its two sides—before God and in man—so deliverance has its two sides too. Sin has its penalty and power, therefore salvation consists of two sides as well. Yet this is not two deliverances but two sides of *one* deliverance. The Lord saves us from the fear of penalty, the accusation of the conscience, and all agitations; at the same time, He delivers us from the power of sin. And thus His salvation is complete. He saves us from the penalty imposed by God and He delivers us from the power of sin in us.

How does the Lord die for us in order to affect these two sides of sin? The Bible tells us that he who sins must die. But the sinless Lord Jesus bore the penalty of death for us. He shed His blood to redeem us and to wash away all our sins before God. The blood of Christ has washed us. It is most amazing that the Bible never says that the blood of Christ washed our heart. Hebrews 9.14 observes this: "How much more shall the blood of Christ, who through the eternal Spirit offered himself without blemish unto God, cleanse your conscience from dead works to serve the living God?" Notice that it does not say the blood cleanses the heart, it only cleanses the conscience.

What is the conscience? It is that which accuses within us, telling us we are wrong, therefore deserving of death and perdition. The blood of Christ cleanses our conscience so that we are no longer being accused by it, thus securing peace. His blood causes us to know that although our sins are worthy of punishment, Christ has died for these sins and has fulfilled the righteousness of God. However, no one by the cleansing of the blood is transformed to be morally good and sin no more, thereby becoming free from sin. For the blood of Christ can only cleanse us before God and eliminate the accusation of the conscience; it does not wash our heart and make it so clean that sin no longer is hidden in us. The blood of the Lord is objective, not subjective, in its effect. It does not cleanse the heart; it cleanses the conscience.

Men are all defiled and corrupted. Through the blood of Christ, sins are forgiven and the *penalty* of sins is paid. But the Bible never tells us that the blood can eradicate the *power* of sin. This is that other side of which we spoke earlier. The word of God tells us, on the one side, of the blood of Christ and on the other side, of the cross of Christ. Blood speaks of death, and so, too, does the cross. Yet blood is related to penalty, for it deals with man's sins before God; but the cross deals with the power of sin within us. It is through the cross that our heart is purified and is made capable of overcoming sin.

Let us reiterate the difference between the cross and the blood. The blood of Christ takes away our sins before God, whereas the cross of Christ deals with the sin that is in us. Be aware, however, that the cross does not *crucify* the sin in us. Many advocates of holiness err here. The cross of Christ does not crucify sin. Nowhere in the Scripture can anyone find a verse saying that the cross crucifies sin. Then what *does* the cross crucify? The Lord was crucified on it. The Bible also says our old man was crucified there as well. It was not the powerful sin that was crucified, but it was the old man—who loved to be directed by sin—that was crucified. It was not the root of sin which was eradicated, but it was the old man—who was so intimate with the root of sin—that was crucified by the Lord. Let me tell you the good news today: that when Christ was crucified, not only He himself was crucified, but God also had the corrupted and defiled you and me crucified with Him. We *were* crucified with Him!

"Knowing this, that our old man was crucified with him, that the body of sin might be done away, that so we should no longer be in bondage to sin" (Rom. 6.6). Notice that what is said here is that the old man was crucified with Christ, not that sin was crucified with Him. Have you not heard people say that sin may be crucified or that the root of sin may be eradicated? Let us recognize that there is no such thing.

In this verse in Romans, we see three things: (1) the old man; (2) the body of sin—that is to say, the body that sins; and (3) sin. It also tells us of three important matters: (1) that our old man was crucified with Christ, (2) that the aim was that the body of sin might be done away, and (3) that the result would be that I should no longer be in bondage to sin. Thus, with the old man crucified, I should no longer sin nor will to sin. But sin itself will not have died, sin itself is yet alive.

Let me illustrate it as follows: Here are the three things: the old man, sin, and the body of sin. Sin is like a master, the old man is like a steward, and the body is like a puppet. Sin has no authority nor power to direct the body of sin to sin. As a master, sin directs the old man, and with the consent of the old man the body is made a puppet. As long as the old man is alive, it stands between the body at the outside and sin on the inside. When the inward sin tempts the old man and stirs up its lusts, the old man gives an order to the body to commit sin. The body is rather weak; it will do whatever it is made to do. It has no sovereignty of its own, nor can it do anything on its own. It does whatever the old man orders it to do. Now though, the Lord comes to rescue us. He does not kill our body nor does He eradicate the root of sin, He instead has our old man crucified with Him.

Consequently, only two out of the three things

mentioned in Romans 6.6 are left; the body is at the outside and sin is on the inside. But now, in the middle, a new person has taken over the position formerly held by the old man. So that today in order to induce the body to sin, the sin within must come to tempt the new man, trying to stir up lust; but the new man will not listen to it nor agree with its suggestion. Formerly the old man contemplated a love and desire for sin; but now the new man will have nothing to do with sin nor will it respond to its demand. And thus, the body is not able to practice sin.

Let us look at Romans 6.6 further. We know that sin is most corrupt in its nature, so we all hope to have it eradicated from our body. Nevertheless, we do not realize that the existence of the root of sin or the existence of the devil actually has nothing to do with whether or not we bear the fruit of holiness in our lives. What is actually at the bottom of it all is our old man. Each time we find ourselves tempted, stirred and committed to sin, it is all because our old man is alive. However, the Lord has already had our old man crucified with Him.

What is the aim of having the old man crucified? It is just this: "that the body of sin might be done away." In the original Greek, the word translated "done away" actually means "disemployed"; which signifies that without the old man, the body of sin is disabled from doing anything. Formerly the body of sin daily worked according to the order of the old man. Sinning appeared to be its profession. Apart from sinning, the body seems to have had nothing else to do because the old man loved sin too much; and hence, the body simply followed suit and became the body of sin. But now the old man has been dealt with by the Lord by it having been crucified with Him on the cross, and thus the body of sin has become unemployed. Formerly, when the old man was still alive, the body of sin daily sinned as though sinning was its profession, its job. Thank the Lord, the irrepressible old man, the old man of you and me, has been crucified! And the body of sin is now unemployed! Even though sin still exists and attempts to be master, yet you and I are no longer its bondman. In spite of its repeated efforts to cause the body to sin, the new man, under the dominion of the Holy Spirit, will not cooperate. Consequently, sin has now no way to cause the body to sin. The Bible shows us that the result of having the old man crucified and the body of sin unemployed is "that so we should no longer be in bondage to sin."

The old man is dead; therefore, we can overcome sin completely. The blood of Christ was shed to save us from our sins before God and to cleanse our conscience from accusation. It tells us that we are now no longer people of perdition but are those instead who have peace with God. However, if we only know this aspect of salvation, our daily living will still be miserable. Though we know our sins are forgiven, we yet continue to make sinning our profession. We still cannot overcome sin in our daily living, nor can we bear the fruit of holiness. We are forced to sin daily; we have no peace in our hearts; and our communion with God is frequently interrupted. We know we are saved and have eternal life, but such sinning daily deprives us of the joy of salvation. Thank God, though, that the salvation of the Lord is no half-way measure. The Lord sheds His blood to cleanse us from our sins, and His cross sets aside the old man and delivers us from the power of sin.

Please be assured continually of this fact that each believer is dead as to the old man, yet not by his committing suicide. Some preach that each Christian ought to put himself to death in order not to sin again. Such counsel, however, is an error, simply because that at the time when the Lord Jesus was crucified, He brought us to the cross with Him as well. Let me ask you today if you are dead. Let me say that you and I can thank the Lord together for His having already crucified this hard-to-deal-with and impossible-to-kill old man of ours. Thank and praise the Lord! Hallelujah!

I wonder if we really know how utterly corrupted we are! I know I am most corrupted. How many times I was oppressed by the power of sin; how I longed that I would die. But sadly I could not put myself to death. Later on, I began to see that when the Lord was crucified, He put my old man to death with Him that the body of sin might no longer be in bondage to sin. And how happy I am today! Due to the work of Christ, sin has been trampled beneath my feet, for it now has no power over me. I praise and thank the Lord!

Please recognize that your sin cannot be gotten rid of through prayer, Bible reading, piety, worship, self-restraint, or suffering. It is only the Lord who can do this, and who has already done it when He took your old man with Him to the cross that you might be delivered. Always remember this: that the blood deals with our sins before God while the cross deals with the old man.

What, then, should be our attitude toward sin? "Even so reckon ye also yourselves to be dead unto sin, but alive unto God in Christ Jesus" (Rom. 6.11). Some think we should reckon sin to be dead; but let me tell you that it is not a matter of reckoning sin as dead but one of reckoning self as having already been crucified.

However, many believers do not understand why it is that their experience does not bear out the fact that since the Lord has already had their old man crucified, their body of sin ought today to be unemployed and that they should no longer be in bondage to sin in their daily lives. Yet they still continue to sin, they still are not freed from the dominion of sin, and their body is still busily driven to commit sins. Why is this so? It is because in spite of what the Lord has accomplished for us in His perfect salvation, we have not yet accepted His work and believed in what He has accomplished, and taken His victory by faith. He has indeed crucified our old man, but we have not single-mindedly believed that the old man was crucified, for we continue to consider our old man to be alive.

It is in view of this very situation that Paul after telling us in Romans 6.6 the fact of salvation, shows us in Romans 6.11 what we should do. Romans 6.6 states that our old man was crucified; verse 11 reasons that if the Lord has already had the old man crucified, then we must now reckon it as truly dead, thus unable to force us any longer to sin. We may now therefore say to sin: my old man is dead, I am consequently no longer your slave. It is impossible for us ever to see sin die or our lusts die. Sin is far more vigilant and active than we are. And as soon as there is opportunity, it will attempt to lay its hand on us. It will never die. Nevertheless, it need not be feared, for our old man is dead. We may overcome sin not by our reckoning sin to be dead, but by *believing* the accomplished work of Christ in our reckoning our old man to be dead indeed.

How do we reckon? Perhaps a basic lesson in arithmetic can be helpful here. Two plus two equals four. Why do we reckon it as four? Simply because two plus two is really four. Hence the command of Romans 6.11 to reckon ourselves to be dead does not at all mean to imply—much like the Chinese proverb which says, "Consider yourself as having died yesterday"—that we, not really having died, are nonetheless to imagine ourselves as dead. No, the death of our old man has already been carried out by God; therefore, we reckon it as indeed most real. Reckoning simply means that since *God* has reckoned me as crucified, I therefore also reckon myself to be dead. I reckon two plus two as four because it is neither three nor five but in truth four. God says I was crucified; I believe this word, so I acknowledge myself to be dead. Faith is merely saying what God himself has said. God has declared my sins have been forgiven, so I also declare my sins have truly been forgiven. God has declared I have died, hence I too acknowledge and declare myself to have died. Christians who stand daily on the ground of what God has said in Romans 6 are able to overcome all sins. There is not a single sin which cannot be overcome, because the Lord has crucified our old man.

Buried

Now let us return to our original subject of baptism. Why are we baptized? The cleansing of sin is one side, and I being dead is the other side. Since my sins have been washed clean, I should be baptized to testify to the fact of sins cleansed. But then, too, because my old man is dead, I should also be baptized to testify to the fact that my old man is actually dead. What is the first thing done after death? Would anyone retain the corpse many days for viewing? After so many days the corpse will probably start to decay. Last year a sister among us died. We really missed her, but we could not retain her body. Since a person is dead, there is no use for the dead body, and so we bury it. Burying testifies to the fact that the buried one is dead.

Suppose you have a dear one whom you love as your own self. But he is sick almost unto death. He still exhibits some pulse and some breath, though he lies motionless and speechless. Would you put him in a coffin? No you would not. Why? Because you do not believe he is dead. When do you bury your most beloved parents, wife, or friend? Only when you know he or she is dead and cannot ever live anymore do you bury that person. If there is a thread of hope, you will not bury that one. But after the loved one is dead and beyond hope, you can do nothing more but to bury that person.

The Bible tells us that after our co-crucifixion with Christ we need to be buried with Him too. The biblical meaning of baptism is not only a cleansing but also a burial. We must be baptized because in so doing we testify to the fact that we believe we are dead. Hence we ask someone to bury us beneath the waters of baptism. This confirms our belief that we have died. Anyone who does not believe that he is dead should not be baptized. For this would be a burying him alive! He who is baptized must believe he was crucified with Christ. How do you express your faith? How do you testify to the completed work of Christ? Through baptism. When you are buried in the water and are baptized, you express your faith (1) in the cleansing of your sins through the blood of Christ and (2) in the co-crucifixion of your old man with Christ on the cross. You believe the fact; therefore, you receive baptism to prove you are now cleansed and dead.

Hence the condition of baptism is two-fold. The Bible not only tells us to rise up and be baptized to wash away our sins because we believe God has already atoned for our sins and cleansed them; it also tells us to rise up and be buried in the water because we believe we are dead. Not only sins washed away, but also the person buried out of sight. Sins are washed away, and the person is likewise washed away. Such is the meaning as well as the testimony of baptism.

Final Words

As you read this, are you able to bear such testimony? I really have no need to persuade you to be baptized. If you have not yet believed in the Lord Jesus and your sins have not been forgiven, I hope you will quickly believe. If you *have* believed but still are ignorant that sin can be completely overcome, then you ought to know that our Lord has already had you crucified with Him. Now, nothing can tempt you to sin, for you can overcome all sins. With a believing heart, stand on Romans 6, believing yourself to be dead. What can sin therefore do to you? Believers must stand on Romans 6.6 and 6.11 in order to overcome sin. Reckon yourself to be dead, then prayer and Bible reading will be effective.

Anyone who believes the blood of Christ has cleansed him of his sins and also believes his old man was crucified with Christ, let him rise up and be baptized.

6 Confess Sin

And Jehovah spake unto Moses, saying, If any one sin, and commit a trespass against Jehovah, and deal falsely with his neighbor in a matter of deposit, or of bargain, or of robbery, or have oppressed his neighbor, or have found that which was lost, and dealt falsely therein, and swear to a lie; in any of all these things that a man doeth, sinning therein; then it shall be, if he hath sinned, and is guilty, that he shall restore that which he took by robbery, or the thing which he hath gotten by oppression, or the deposit which was committed to him, or the lost thing which he found, or any thing about which he hath sworn falsely; he shall even restore it in full, and shall add the fifth part more thereto: unto him to whom it appertaineth shall he give it, in the day of his being found guilty. (Lev. 6.1–5)

Blessed is he whose transgression is forgiven, whose sin is covered. Blessed is the man unto whom Jehovah imputeth not iniquity, and in whose spirit there is no guile. When I kept silence, my bones wasted away through my groaning all the day long. For day and night thy hand was heavy upon me: my moisture was changed as with the drought of summer. I acknowledged my sin unto thee, and my iniquity did I not hide: I said, I will confess my transgressions unto Jehovah; and thou forgavest the iniquity of my sin. For this let every one that is godly pray unto thee in a time when thou mayest be found: surely when the great waters overflow they shall not reach unto him. Thou art my hiding-place; thou wilt preserve me from trouble; thou wilt compass me about with songs of deliverance. (Ps. 32.1–7)

He that covereth his transgressions shall not prosper; but whoso confesseth and forsaketh them shall obtain mercy. (Prov. 28.13)

If therefore thou art offering thy gift at the altar, and there rememberest that thy brother hath ought against thee, leave there thy gift before the altar, and go thy way, first be reconciled to thy brother, and then come and offer thy gift. Agree with thine adversary quickly, while thou art with him in the way; lest haply the adversary deliver thee to the judge, and the judge deliver thee to the officer, and thou be cast into prison. Verily I say unto thee, Thou shalt by no means come out thence, till thou have paid the last farthing. (Matt. 5.23–26)

But when he saw many of the Pharisees and Sadducees coming to his baptism, he said unto them, Ye offspring of vipers, who warned you to flee from the wrath to come? Bring forth therefore fruit worthy of repentance. (Matt. 3.7,8)

And the multitudes asked him, saying, What then must we do? And he answered and said unto them, He

> that hath two coats, let him impart to him that hath none; and he that hath food, let him do likewise. And there came also publicans to be baptized and they said unto him, Teacher, what must we do? And he said unto them, Extort no more than that which is appointed you. And soldiers also asked him, saying, And we, what must we do? And he said unto them, Extort from no man by violence, neither accuse any one wrongfully; and be content with your wages. (Luke 3.10–14)

Why do we deal with this problem of confessing sin? Because this is an important thing to do after a person is saved. First of all, let us be clear on one point, that no Christian anywhere in the world is saved by the confession of his sin. Some people teach that without confession of sin there is no salvation. This is heresy. No one is saved by such confession. This is putting the cart before the horse. The order cannot be reversed in salvation. Some others declare that the amount of forgiveness is directly proportional to the amount of confession of sin. This too is heresy, for it transforms the glorious work of Christ into dust and ashes. We hear people say if the eye sins, crucify the eye, that it may be purified from sin. Once a person told me, Mr. So-and-So preached the word of the cross. I asked him whose cross did he preach? Paul declared, "I determined not to know anything among you, save Jesus Christ, and him crucified" (1 Cor. 2.2). It is not your cross; it is His cross. Your cross cannot save you, but the cross of the Lord Jesus can. If we crucify our eye, that will be our cross, not the cross of Christ. Yet it is Christ who bore our sin on the cross. Without His death, we can never be saved.

For this reason, it is not our confession of sin which saves us. I do not say we have no need to confess our sin; but let us be careful in distinguishing the first step from the second step. Let us see that salvation precedes confession. First be saved, and then confess sin. That which saves us is nothing but the precious blood of the Lord Jesus. I am not overlooking confession of sin, but I would uplift the Lord Jesus. Our salvation is not based on confession of sin, but on the precious blood of the Lord Jesus Christ.

Confessing sin is not directly related to salvation; it is immediately related to reward. Matthew 5.23–26 says that if you remember that your brother has anything against you, the first thing you need to do is to be reconciled to him. You should earnestly seek for reconciliation lest he deliver you to the judge, who in turn delivers you to the officer for your confinement in prison. This tells us how this Christian will suffer loss in the kingdom when Christ shall rule on earth for a thousand years. Hence let us be very clear that a Christian is saved through the Lord Jesus, but if he fails to confess his sins after salvation he will suffer loss during the kingdom age.

The Necessity of Confessing Sin

"He that covereth his transgressions shall not prosper; but whoso confesseth and forsaketh them shall obtain mercy" (Prov. 28.13). Let us be those who confess the sins which we committed in the past. Let us apologize to men if we have sinned against them. Let us confess to God if we have offended Him. Otherwise we may suffer loss in the future.

Once when Evan Roberts was asked about spiritual growth, he answered, "When did you last confess your sin?" The one who heard this did not understand what was meant. He wondered how one could confess his sin as though it were a daily affair. Was it like taking meals every day? He recalled that he had not confessed his sins for many years now. Subsequently, he came to know what Mr. Roberts had meant. He too began to see that a Christian makes progress as he confesses his sins. We must confess to God when God is offended and confess to men when man is offended; and this will thus enable us Christians to grow in spiritual life.

How many feel sorrowful after they have sinned? If people do not feel sorrowful, this indicates they have failed in the matter of confessing sin. But if any Christian will clear up his sins against God and men with confession, he will proceed well in the course which is before him. He will walk faster than other Christians. How sad that many believers have too little sensitivity toward sin.

Many dare not sin for the sake of saving face, either for their own reputation or for the reputation of their family. Some dare not sin because they do not have the capital to sin (that is to say, they lack the ability or opportunity). Some others dare not sin for fear of its consequence. But let me ask you, How many of you do not dare to sin because of its hatefulness, uncleanness, and opposition to God? I am surprised at finding people sleeping soundly and eating well after they have committed sins. Our God hates sin. I hate sin not because of saving face, or lack of capital or fear of its consequence, but because of God. In order to sharpen their sensitivity toward sin, let Christians confess their sins. I can say at the very least that confessing sin will help us to hate sin.

Is there any controversy between you and other people? In the diary of Pastor Cook, it was written; "There is nothing between me and men, I now have nothing to repent, nothing to recompence; I am prepared to die." Can we also say that we have confessed all our sins? Is there anyone who has yet to make confession? How often people dare not settle accounts. This by itself unveils the fact that there is something wrong. As we are about to eat a pear and notice a small hole in the skin, we sense that something may be wrong inside that fruit. We may want to eat the pear, but we are afraid to open it up.

The Scope of Confessing Sin

The scope of confession is governed by the scope of sin. Do not confess more than the scope of sin, nor confess less than its scope. If the scope of my sin is that I have offended God, I must confess to God as my scope of confession. But if I sin against both God and a certain brother, then my scope of confession must include both God and that brother. It is therefore unwise to confess openly to the public what I have sinned against God or against another person. In many revival meetings, people are asked to confess their sins in public. This is a mistake, for it only defiles many minds. Confess to one person if the sin is against one person; confess to five persons, if the sin is against five persons. On the other hand, the scope of confession should not be less than the scope of sin. If I sin against God and also against another brother, it is not acceptable just to confess to God and not to that brother. As the scope of sin is, so shall be the scope of confession. Confession ought not be any wider or narrower than those who have been offended by the sin.

The Consequence of Confessing Sin

Concerning this matter of confessing sin, let me tell you a little of my past experience. In my youth, I studied in a mission school. I usually got ninety to a hundred—with an average mark of ninety-five—in all my examinations except one: I could not pass my Bible course (I having had absolutely no interest in this Book). Thus my overall average was lowered by this one failure. During my third year, I began to figure that in spite of the fact that I disliked the Bible (at that time I was not yet saved), it was not very profitable for me for my teachers to have to report that I was excellent in all courses except this one. So I decided to really study this Book. It happened that we were studying the book of Acts that semester. I prepared for the upcoming examination by spending several months in studying Acts; yet my determination to pass *par excellence* was so strong that I wrote the important points of that Bible book on my arm, which was then covered by my long sleeve. I of course answered all the questions well. My grade turned out to be over seventy (formerly I had achieved a mark of only forty to fifty).

Later on, I was saved. I felt uneasy about this cheating episode, but I dared not confess lest my teacher and the principal should think that I got all my good marks in the other subjects through cheating. I was also afraid that I would be expelled from the school since the rule of the school was to expel immediately all who cheated. Furthermore, I had already incurred the displeasure of the principal because I had disagreed with the Anglican Church on certain truths which they held. I was really apprehensive about facing my parents if I were indeed expelled. Thus I struggled for not a few days till I finally realized that without confession I would never have peace. My conscience might sleep; but it would never die. As a result, I wrote to the principal and confessed my sin. The principal called me in and told me that on behalf of the school he forgave my sin.

Many times our conscience may slumber, but when it wakes up, it will always remind us of the sin unconfessed. A sin that is unconfessed leaves a scar. Your conscience may be silenced, yet it cannot be silenced forever. He who confesses his sin will alone have peace. Let me tell you, the taste of sin is like the taste of hell. How often men will cry out like David: "When I kept silence, my bones wasted away through my groaning all the day long. For day and night thy hand was heavy upon me: my moisture was changed as with the drought of summer." But after he confessed his sin, David declared: "thou wilt compass me about with songs of deliverance."

We have touched upon the losing of sensitivity toward sin by not confessing it; we will now deal with the fact of losing joy if sin is not confessed. Some may raise the question why there is no joy in them after being saved. Some people have no joy because they do not witness for the Lord; some, because they are disobedient on certain matters; some, because they are not willing to give up certain things. Others, however, do not have joy because they do not confess their sin. The joy that comes with the confessing of sin is great.

Once I was conducting meetings at Chuanchow (a city in Fukien Province). The principal of a certain school there intended to bring a group of grade school pupils to the meeting. I was somewhat taken aback for fear that they would interfere with the meeting. But this principal was a person of experience. He believed in the power of the gospel that it would probably save some of the young ones. Later on, a teacher from that same school told me that something had happened in the school. Upon inquiry, I was told that the wind of confessing sin was blowing strong there. It all began with a seven-year-old child who with some other pupils had once stolen some fruit from the tree next to the principal's office. At the time, the child well knew it was a sin. He wanted to confess, but he was afraid of the principal. Yet he could not get peace if he did not confess. He cried for two days until finally he confessed to the principal.

The same teacher also related to me several other cases that had occurred at the school. Among these cases was the story of a child about eleven years old. Several years ago, he had seen his fellow students buying candy outside the gate of the school. He himself had no money to buy any candy. Then he remembered having seen several pennies lying on the table of a particular teacher's bedroom. He stealthily entered the room and took six pennies for the candy. He now was very much troubled by this sin. He thought of recompense, but he had no money. So he asked his sister for six pennies. His sister pressed him for a reason, but he would not give it. He insisted he must have the money, and so he was given the pennies. But the sister secretly spied out his next movements: he took the money to that teacher and confessed his past sin. Let me say that it is absolutely necessary to confess sin. A sin that is unconfessed will follow you throughout your life. Take note of what Moses said: "Your sin will find you out" (Num. 32.23b). Sin does not sit still nor is it afar. It will follow you and find you out.

It so happened that I related some of these stories from the platform on the next day. After the meeting, some judges who had attended came to me and remarked: "According to what you told us in your message, there will be no need of us judges. If people will voluntarily return what they steal, there will be no need of courts. Although we have not yet embraced Christianity, we can see through these instances the true character of Christianity"!

Confessing sin will not only give peace and joy, it

will also gain the person or persons whom you have offended. Even the hardest one among your friends will break down in tears and confess Jesus as his Savior if you confess to him with tears your sin against him and also your faith in the Lord Jesus. I have had just such an experience myself. Who in the world will do such a thing if there is no Christ?

Do you have any sin which needs to be confessed? Do it quickly. It certainly is not an easy task. Sometimes I have agonized for weeks, for months, before I confessed. Perhaps you are better than I, but within the first year after I was saved I confessed over a hundred sins. Have you offended anybody? Get right with them by confessing your sin.

Yet, besides obtaining peace and joy and gaining people, confessing sin enables us to witness for the Lord. Without it, there can be no testimony. Suppose I do not confess my sin; would you not question the credibility of my preaching? We must confess our sins, we must judge our sins more than judging others. Then shall our testimony be effective. Otherwise, we can neither persuade people nor bear witness to them.

Restitution

Confessing sin is one thing, restitution is another. Is there anything in your house which is not justly yours? It may have come into your possession through unrighteous means. You may have stolen it or picked it up on the street, or it may be a debt that has not yet been repaid. Are you willing to clear it up at your first opportunity? If not, how can you expect God to bless you? Many Christians are rather careless about such matters. According to Leviticus, you must not only return the principal but also add one fifth to it as interest. You must not defraud anybody. Rather, you should be willing to be defrauded yourself than to defraud others. This is a basic Christian attitude.

In case the person you trespass against is no longer living, restore it to his family. And if there is no family, give it to the priest. If the defrauded person were still living, the priest could not at all take the restitution. And this is still applicable today. Once a maid stole something worth about sixty dollars from her mistress. She later was saved and realized her sin. So she saved seventy dollars. One day she brought the money to a servant of the Lord and asked him to use it for God's work. Upon inquiry, it was discovered that her mistress was still living. So she was told she should take the money to her mistress and confess her sin, she being strongly reprimanded that God would never use stolen money for His work.

If anyone has trespassed against people in material things, he should find the original owner and restore it to him. If the owner is not living, it should be returned to his family. If there is no family, then give it to the church. Oh, let us allow God to dig deep into our lives. James has told us this: "Confess therefore your sins one to another" (James 5.16a). You are not held responsible for the sins you have forgotten, but you *are* responsible for the sins you remember. May there not be anyone who will wait till tomorrow to hear again the word of God.

7 | Communion with God and Enlightenment

And they shall make an ark of acacia wood; two cubits and a half shall be the length thereof, and a cubit and a half the breadth thereof, and a cubit and a half the height thereof. And thou shalt overlay it with pure gold, within and without shalt thou overlay it, and shalt make upon it a crown of gold round about. And thou shalt cast four rings of gold for it, and put them in the four feet thereof; and two rings shall be on the one side of it, and two rings on the other side of it. And thou shalt make staves of acacia wood, and overlay them with gold. And thou shalt put the staves into the rings on the sides of the ark, wherewith to bear the ark. The staves shall be in the rings of the ark: they shall not be taken from it. And thou shalt put into the ark the testimony which I shall give thee. And thou shalt make a mercy-seat of pure gold: two cubits and a half shall be the length thereof, and a cubit and a half the breadth thereof. And thou shalt make two cherubim of gold: of beaten work shalt thou make them at the two ends of the

> mercy-seat. And make one cherub at the one end, and one cherub at the other end: of one piece with the mercy-seat shall ye make the cherubim on the two ends thereof. And the cherubim shall spread out their wings on high, covering the mercy-seat with their wings, with their faces one to another; toward the mercy-seat shall the faces of the cherubim be. And thou shalt put the mercy-seat above upon the ark; and in the ark thou shalt put the testimony that I shall give thee. And there I will meet with thee, and I will commune with thee from above the mercy-seat, from between the two cherubim which are upon the ark of the testimony, of all things which I will give thee in commandment unto the children of Israel. (Ex. 25.10–22)

The Mercy-Seat and the Cherubim

"And there will I meet with thee, and I will commune with thee from above the mercy-seat, from between the two cherubim which are upon the ark of the testimony, of all things which I will give thee in commandment unto the children of Israel" (v.22). Two things are distinctly touched upon here: one is communion, the other is enlightenment. "There I will meet with thee"—this is communion. "I will commune with thee from above the mercy-seat, from between the two cherubim . . . of all things . . . in commandment"—this is enlightenment.

In the Old Testament period, the one thing which God paid most attention to was His tabernacle, which became the temple later on. This was because God had a great purpose as well as a great expectation of dwelling among His own people. What He has always desired is to tabernacle among men. In other words, the primary matter in the eternal purpose of God is that He may abide in the midst of men. The great pleasure of God is to have a point of contact between Him and humanity. This is why the Lord Jesus is "the Word [that] became flesh, and dwelt among us . . ., full of grace and truth" (John 1.14). "Dwelt among us" may be translated "tabernacled among us." God's purpose is to dwell among us. The name Immanuel is employed to demonstrate the fact of God with man. Yet the Lord Jesus is only one person in whom God dwells. But through Him and by His spirit He also will build us into "a habitation of God in the Spirit" (Eph. 2.22).

The center of the tabernacle or temple is the ark of covenant. Whenever the ark left the tabernacle, the latter became something forsaken. Whenever the ark was taken into captivity, the temple was no longer God's habitation. For in the olden days God dwelt with men by means of the ark, and men communed with God also through the ark. Here we are not able to present the entire meaning of the ark for it is too big a subject to deal with. We would rather touch upon just one thing, which is the mercy-seat above the ark with the two cherubim of gold—of beaten work—at the two ends of the mercy-seat. God would meet Moses from above the mercy-seat between the two cherubim, and there He would speak to him. We shall now consider this matter of how God communed with men from above the mercy-seat between the two cherubim, and also of how He spoke to men that they might be enlightened.

Communion

The mercy-seat was where God dispensed His mercy. Each year on the tenth of the seventh month, on the day of atonement, the blood of the sin-offering would be sprinkled on the mercy-seat (Lev. 16.14,15). In other words, upon the mercy-seat was where sins were atoned. Hence, from this we can see that all the many graces of God are given to men only after sins are atoned. Without the remission of sins, men can never expect any mercy from God. The blood of the sin-offering had to be sprinkled upon the golden mercy-seat before God could show mercy to men. The natural concept of men is that God has the authority to dispense grace and that He can show mercy whenever He desires to do so. God's intention is indeed to show grace; otherwise, He would never have set up the mercy-seat of old. But let us see that unless on the annual day of atonement the blood had been sprinkled on the mercy-seat by the Jewish high priest, God could not forgive anybody's sins.

At the two ends of the mercy-seat were the cherubim. The glory of God is above the cherubim (see Ez. 9.3, Heb. 9.5). On the mercy-seat man meets the mercies of God, and between the two cherubim man sees the glory of God. In other words, the mercy of God must agree with the glory of God. He would never have set up the mercy-seat without also the cherubim. God would never have dispensed grace from the mercy seat and by-passed the cherubim. It is true that God today could treat us with grace from His mercy-seat because He loves to be gracious to us; yet He chooses not to deal with us according to His mercy-seat alone, but deals with us according to the cherubim as well. Since men have all sinned and come short of the glory of God, men and God's glory are no longer compatible. If God should deal with us according to His glory, none of us could receive the grace of God. We would be cursed and forsaken. There was therefore the need for the blood of atonement to be sprinkled on the mercy-seat in olden times. Only thus could God deal with man according to both glory and the mercy-seat.

All this should cause us to see one thing—that our communion with God today is based upon our suitability with God's glory. And such suitability can come only from the blood. Because of the blood God can show grace without jeopardizing His glory. Let all children of God be cognizant of this one fact: whoever approaches God must not compromise His glory. If in drawing near to the Lord anyone brings with him something which falls short of the glory of God, he can have no communion with Him. For the basis of communion is God's glory. Many brothers and sisters do indeed testify that communion is based on the blood. But let us understand that this is so because communion by its very nature involves God's glory. If God's glory were not involved, there would be no demand for the blood. But it is necessary to have the blood during the time of communion because God is the God of glory.

In the third chapter of Romans we are told on the one hand that we all have sinned and fallen short of the glory of God, and on the other hand that we are justified by the blood of Jesus. Since God is a glorious God, whoever comes before Him must remember that his communion with Him is governed by his current attitude towards God's glory. Whatever deprives God of His glory is sin; whatever desecrates God's glory is sin. Sin hinders us from having communion with God. It is not necessary for us to commit some particularly hideous sin to hinder our communion with Him. No, if we do not actively glorify God in *anything,* our communion with Him can suffer. We need to always remember that our communion with God is based on His glory as well as on the blood. The glory of God demands the blood. If we had not fallen short of the glory of God, we would need no blood. But we *have* fallen short of His glory, and therefore we must have the blood. Thus glory is, in the final analysis, the basis of communion, while blood is added to remedy the lack of such glory.

Let us understand that though communion is interrupted by sin, sin is only something negative. It does not really explain the fundamental problem, which is desecration of the glory of God. Whenever we come short of God's glory, we have a problem with communion. Thank God, today there is blood on the mercy-seat—that is to say, there is blood on the cross of Calvary. By the blood of Jesus, we can behold God's glory and even live in His glory. Thank the Lord, because His redemption has placed us in a position whereby we may uphold the glory of God with unveiled face. This is communion. Communion is not limited to half an hour or an hour of prayer and Bible reading. It is to behold the glory of God through the blood of the Lamb and to live for His glory.

Enlightenment

The next thing to be perceived from Leviticus 25.22 is the fact of God speaking, or, to put it another way, the fact of the enlightenment or revelation of God. God spoke to Moses from the mercy-seat between the two cherubim. In the realm of *communion*, the emphasis is on the mercy-seat for there God met with Moses. Yet the Lord in His word does not permit us to overlook the cherubim—which in fact represent His glory. In the realm of *enlightenment*, the emphasis is on the cherubim, for God spoke to Moses from between them, though again He does not allow us to neglect the mercy-seat either. If we can commune with God at the mercy-seat, we shall be able to hear His word coming out from between the cherubim.

God spoke to Moses from between the two cherubim. He, as it were, used His glory to guide the children of Israel. Where the glory of God was, there was His guidance. In the daytime, it was the pillar of cloud; in the nighttime, it was the pillar of fire. In the pillar of fire as well as in the pillar of cloud, people can see the glory of God.

Hence, God speaks and guides today according to His glory. When God speaks, we know He is to be glorified in that particular matter. If we are able to see His glory in any matter, we know we already have His guidance there. Unfortunately, in the lives of many children of God, guidance and glorifying God become two separate things. Who of us knows that before God our glorifying of Him and His guiding of us are in reality one thing? For wherever we find the glory of God, it is to there that we are led. Where God's glory is, there we should be also.

God spoke in ancient times from between the two cherubim. Whoever today sees the glory of God, he has heard God's word. We have no need to wait for his word once we have seen His glory. If once in life we see His glory, such a sight gives us much deeper understanding than we ordinarily have. Whenever we see the glory of God, we are "in the know."

Right or wrong, straight or crooked, spiritually valuable or unvaluable—all these are measured by the presence or absence of God's glory. Certain matters may be minute and insignificant in human eyes, yet at times when you touch these you touch the very glory of God. And as you touch His glory, you know you already have obtained His guidance. You have no need to wait anymore. While doing some works you may sense little worth or that something is not quite right in them, whereas other works you are engaged in make you feel they are worthwhile and intrinsically right. The problem lies not in the outward greatness or smallness of the work; it hinges instead upon the presence or absence of the glory of God: *without* God's glory, no value; *with* His glory, much value.

Moses came forth to deliver God's word. Because he had the ministry of the word, he could serve the people of God with the word. Whatever God commanded Moses to deliver to the children of Israel came from between the two cherubim. So that when Moses spoke for God, he had already touched the glory of God. In like manner, today, if we have seen and touched God's glory, we shall have words to deliver. Sometimes you may reckon yourself as speaking well, but you sense a kind of levity and frivolity within. If so, you shall at once discern that there is not the witness of the word nor the ministry of the word. Anything which comes from God comes from between the two cherubim, hence you are subjectively aware of the glory of God. God's glory is not merely an objective thing—it can veritably be known in us.

Often in your daily life you touch God's glory. You see something which will glorify Him and thus you are led by this glory. Many times you touch God's glory in your work. You witness His glory in the work, and hence you conclude that His glory has guided you. When you serve the church with word and you touch the glory of God, you know that what you say is His word. Each time you receive a revelation from God you touch His glory. You have heard Him speak as it were from between the two cherubim. And thus there is not only word but also glory. Whenever there is mere word but no glory, you know that this is only doctrine; but when there is glory as well as word, you know that this is revelation. One thing is rather amazing, which is, that whenever we see God's glory, we know inwardly but we may not be able to utter it adequately. We may be at a loss to explain when being asked, yet the effect is undeniably upon us. The appearing of glory strikes us to the ground. And as we are prostrate upon the ground, we may not comprehend much, but we know we have touched God.

Touching the glory of God is the foundation of enlightenment from, as well as communion with, God. If ever this foundation is lacking, all we have are but doctrines and ideals. May God be gracious to us that daily we may touch His glory and therefore live.

8 Love God

And he said unto him, Thou shalt love the Lord thy God with all thy heart, and with all thy soul, and with all thy mind. This is the great and first commandment. (Matt. 22.37,38)

Some time ago, a missionary died in Fukien Province. I have said many times before that among my acquaintances she was the deepest in the Lord. Because I knew her more than most people, I had the thought of writing her biography. So I began to collect her writings—in both finished and unfinished form. Several days ago I received a package containing her personal effects, among which I found a paper with a few words written on it: "Oh God, I thank you, because of the command saying, Thou shalt love the Lord thy God with all thy heart and with all thy soul, and with all thy mind." How deep is the thought! I wonder how many Christians would say, "O God, I thank You, for You have commanded us to love You with all our hearts and souls and minds"? Because we all are believers we therefore ought to love God. There is no other religion in the whole world that exhorts people to love God. Loving God is a characteristic of Christianity.

The Bible says that whoever believes in the Son has eternal life. Just believe and that is enough. It does not specify that we must believe with all our heart. Simply believe with the heart, and we shall have eternal life. But in loving God, it is written that we must love Him with all our heart, with all our soul, and with all our mind. This is the first and great commandment. However you place it, it is the greatest. Today we will praise God because He has commanded us to love Him.

God delights in our loving Him, for this is good to Him. Just as it is profitable for us to believe in the Lord and have eternal life, so God wants us to love Him as well as to believe in Him; for loving Him is God's gain too.

What will be the resultant phenomena if we really love God? Let us ponder a few of them as revealed in a number of Scripture passages.

One

"Love not the world, neither the things that are in the world. If any man love the world, the love of the Father is not in him" (1 John 2.15). This indicates that loving the Father is something which may either be present inside us or be running away from us. With a heart of loving the Father within us, we are enabled to love the Father. Yet many young people find it difficult to forsake the world. During meetings when they are stirred they seem to have forsaken the world; but at other times they appear to be closely tied to it. For us to really forsake the world, we must have something better in our heart.

Once there was a painting exhibition. Many paintings were good to look at from a distance, but there was one which required viewing of it at close quarters in order to grasp the idea being presented. This was a painting pointing allegorically to a Christian. In the picture there were lying around all kinds of toys which a child loved. Yet that child did not seem to notice any of them; his eyes instead were fixed upon the window before him, and also his hands were stretched forward. Viewing the painting from a distance would suggest nothing at all, but a closer look revealed a beautiful tiny pigeon perched on the window sill. And the caption beneath the painting indicated in so many words that for the sake of wanting that pretty little pigeon the child forsook all the toys. And thus the moral of the picture became obvious: that in order to possess the more excellent thing one must leave the other things. God has not demanded that we cast away anything; He instead puts before us the more excellent. For the sake of possessing the more excellent, we naturally will forsake many lesser things.

Once a young believer stayed with me for two months. He told me he could not forsake the world. He even said to an elderly couple, "You have already enjoyed the good things of the world; you therefore can afford to sacrifice them now. But I cannot." This young man believed in God, yet he could not love Him. We know that by believing, we are delivered from sins; but only by loving God can we be delivered from the world. Oh, let us allow the love of God to enter into us. And as soon as God's love comes in, the world will vanish away.

Two

"If a man say, I love God, and hateth his brother, he is a liar: for he that loveth not his brother whom he hath seen, cannot love God whom he hath not seen" (1 John 4.20). This is a Bible verse familiar to most people, and even some of the unbelievers quote it. Note, however, that this verse does not imply that you are to love the brother in your home, it says to love your brother in Christ. Frequently the attitude and action of many people make it impossible for you to love them; nevertheless, if God's love has entered into you, you *will* be able to love them. It is not just loving the brethren whom you love; it is loving the brethren, period! It is not merely loving those brethren who are lovely, but loving *all* the brethren. If you cannot love the brethren, it is proven that there is not the love of the Father in you. If you have the love of God, you cannot help but love the brethren.

A certain man's father was murdered. He vowed to avenge his father. Now he was also a true Christian. One day as he and the other people were gathering around a large round table to break bread, he discovered that the person who had murdered his father was sitting by his side. Immediately he got up and went out. There was a fierce battle raging within him: whether to kill the enemy or to break bread with him? At that very moment, he was shown by God the love of Christ. He saw how he had originally been God's enemy himself, and yet Christ had saved him. He was immediately melted by the love of Christ. He wiped away his tears, entered back into the room and broke bread with his enemy. And as they came out of the gathering, he no longer looked upon the one who had murdered his father as an enemy but as a brother in the Lord. Consequently, if we truly have the love of God within our hearts, we will love an unlovely brother.

Three

"Hereby we know that we love the children of God, when we love God and do his commandments. For this is the love of God, that we keep his commandments: and his commandments are not grievous" (1 John 5.2,3). Why is it that whoever loves God will keep His commandments? Let us look at John 14.21,23, which says:

(a) "He that hath my commandments and keepeth them, he it is that loveth me" (v.21a). This tells us that if we love the Lord we will keep His commandments. Who can say today that he has kept all the commandments he knows of which God has commanded him? Putting aside those which he does not know, has he kept all the commandments which he knows? The phrase "he that hath my commandments" means he must find out what those commandments are. Many believers are afraid of God's commandments. Many appear to have their ears stuffed so as not to hear. We should know, however, that besides keeping the commandments which God has already commanded us to do, we must seek out those other commandments of His and keep them also. Seeking out God's commandments is minding the things of God which in turn is the true expression of loving God.

(b) "He that loveth me shall be loved of my Father, and I will love him, and will manifest myself unto him" (v.21b). This shows us the benefit we receive by loving God. I have met many renowned persons in Christianity, but I am afraid only a relatively few of them really know God. Many people know how to study the Bible, but they do not know God. They may know the Scriptures, yet they do not know the power of God. Even some of them can preach what they do not understand. Why is this so? Because the Lord has not revealed to them, which means they have not loved the Lord and kept His commandments. There is only one class of people in the world who truly love the Lord, and they are the faithful obedient ones.

If you want to find people who really know the Lord, do not go to famous places to find them. Frequently in secluded places or in small houses there are people who are serving God. When you meet them, you see God there. They are the people whom I admire the moment I see them. But there are many others who have zeal or ability or good deeds, yet I do not see God in them. Once I was asked what I considered to be the overriding characteristic of a certain missionary. I replied that each time I saw her I sensed the presence of God. Such is the revelation of God. Do you remember the great woman in Shunem and how she told her husband about Elisha? "Behold now, I perceive that this is a holy man of God, that passeth by us continually" (2 Kings 4.9). What did Elisha do that left this woman with such an impression? He had not wrought any miracle; nonetheless each time he passed by her house he aroused in the woman a sense of God. Let me ask, do we love the manifestation of God? If we really so love, then let us seek out the commandments of God and keep them.

(c) "If a man love me, he will keep my word: and my Father will love him, and we will come unto him, and make our abode with him" (v.23). God and Christ will be with those who believe, but God and Christ will abide in those who love. Not only present, but dwell. Sometimes we may not sense His presence, yet we have the Lord abiding in us if we faithfully seek the commandments of God.

"Even as the Father hath loved me, I also have loved you: abide ye in my love. If ye keep my commandments, ye shall abide in my love; even as I have kept my Father's commandments, and abide in his love" (John 15.9,10). What does it mean by abiding in the Lord's love? When we were first saved, we truly felt how much the Lord loved us. Yet now, we sense nothing. Though we may still say that the love of the Lord is deep, we nonetheless do not feel anything. If we abide in the Lord's love, we shall always sense His love. To abide in His love is to give opportunity to the Lord. In other words, we are surrounded by His love. When we are opposed and rejected by people, we know how deeply the Lord loves us. We frequently seek out the commandments of God and keep them, thus we abide in His love. Was there any moment on earth when our Lord did not sense the love of the Father? He lived continually in His Father's love. This is because He always kept the commandments of God. In order to abide in the love of the Lord, we must always keep His commandments. With God's love in us, even the most difficult commandment we can keep.

Four

"We know that to them that love God all things work together for good . . ." (Rom. 8.28). Many are quite familiar with this verse. Yet only one class of people will be benefited, and they are those who love God. If anyone does not love God, nothing will work for him for good. For God does not change the "all things," He changes our hearts instead. Though all things remain the same, we will be benefited if we love God. How easy it is for us to blame this or that for what happens to us. Yet if we love God we will not mind it when under unsatisfactory circumstances because we know that all things will work together for good to those who love God.

Five

"As it is written, Things which eye saw not, and ear heard not, and which entered not into the heart of man, whatsoever things God prepared for them that love him. But unto us God revealed them through the Spirit" (1 Cor. 2.9,10a). What do we learn from these two verses? That what God has prepared for those *who believe in Him* is eternal life, but that what things He has prepared specifically for those *who love Him* is yet in the future. Such future blessing is known only to those who love God. This is far better than any good thing men have thus far seen because it is something which no eye has seen before. This is more excellent than anything men have heard of or even thought of, because it is something which has never entered into the heart of man. But now it is revealed to us by the Holy Spirit. In other words, one who loves the Lord may enjoy even in this lifetime the good things which eye has not seen, ear has not heard, and heart has not thought of. When God reveals His glory to you, you will exclaim, How delightful this is! Heavenly glory is so abundant that you feel as though you cannot bear it any more.

Six

"Blessed is the man that endureth temptation; for when he hath been approved, he shall receive the crown of life, which the Lord promised to them that love him" (James 1.12). Often when we think of the crown of life, we contemplate how much work we have to do. Yet here we are told that there is but one condition for gaining the crown of life—which is, to love the Lord. How we lack love towards our God! It seems as if we have lost our first love! How truly sad.

Seven

As told of in John 21, the Lord had asked Peter, "Do you love Me? Feed My lambs." If anyone really loves the Lord, he will be concerned with souls. It is impossible to love the Lord and be totally uninterested in people's souls. You cannot help but love the souls of those who are near to you.

Eight

"If ye loved me, ye would have rejoiced, because I go unto the Father: for the Father is greater than I" (John 14.28b). In loving the Lord, we not only love the brethren and keep God's commandments but also rejoice over the fact that our Lord Jesus has gone to the Father. In other words, we are glad that our Lord Jesus has gone to the Father and has received the glory. Is this too profound for us to comprehend? Many do not understand what glory was bestowed on the Lord as He ascended back to the Father who is greater than He. Lack of understanding this glory hampers people from worshiping God. Unquestionably, we greatly desire to see those whom we love receive glory. And hence, those who love Jesus will rejoice over the return of our Lord back to the Father.

Nine

"He that loveth father or mother more than me is not worthy of me; and he that loveth son or daughter more than me is not worthy of me. And he that doth not take his cross and follow after me, is not worthy of me" (Matt. 10.37,38a). From these two verses we realize that unless we forsake all we cannot love the Lord more. For the sake of loving the Lord people will forsake their parents, wives, children, position and fame. They can forsake all because they have the love of God.

A believer once commented that during worship we ought to sense the loveliness of God as well as the majesty of God. This is indeed well spoken. We draw near to God because of His loveliness. How does God love us? There are many passages in the Scriptures which tell us of the Lord's love towards us. Such as, personally: "Who [Christ] loved me, and gave himself up for me" (Gal. 2.20c); or, corporately: "Christ also loved the church, and gave himself up for it" (Eph. 5.25b). In Romans 5.8b we read: "While we were yet sinners, Christ died for us." In 1 John 4.10 it declares: "Herein is love, not that we loved God, but that he loved us, and sent his Son to be the propitiation for our sins." Where can we find love apart from the cross? And why does the Lord command us to break the bread often? It is because He does not want us to drift away from Him. We seem so prone to forget, so He draws us back. How can we fail to love Him as we remember how miserable we were as sinners and how great was His grace in saving us! The children of Israel recalled in the wilderness the cucumbers and the leeks and the garlic of Egypt, but they forgot how they had suffered as slaves under the oppression of Pharaoh as well as how the Lord had delivered them out of their great afflictions. It appears that their hearts still lingered back in Egypt. If we forget the cross, we will also forget the love of God. If we forget the love of God, we will undoubtedly think of the world.

How can we love the Lord? "I say unto thee, Her sins, which are many, are forgiven; for she loved much: but to whom little is forgiven, the same loveth little" (Luke 7.47). If we remember how our sins were forgiven, we cannot help but love the Lord. The day the cross ever fails to move us, that very day we are fallen. Evan Roberts wept greatly when he realized that he was not moved by the cross; and this went on for several months until God moved him again. But there then followed the great Welsh Revival, the greatest spiritual renewal the world has ever seen. How did it happen that that woman washed the Lord's feet with her tears, wiped them with her hair, and kissed them with her lips? It was because she remembered how all her sins had been forgiven her.

Let us continually stand at the foot of the cross. And even if later we should become spiritually stronger a hundred times more than what we are today, let us always remember how our sins were forgiven us by the Lord.

"If any man loveth not the Lord, let him be anathema. Maranatha" (1 Cor. 16.22). How solemn is this word! Of a truth, if anyone does not love the Lord, he is to be cursed.

"Grace be with all them that love our Lord Jesus Christ with a love incorruptible" (Eph. 6.24). To whom will God give grace? To all those who love the Lord with a true heart. If anyone should ask you if you believe in the Lord, you will surprise the whole world if your answer is, "I love the Lord."

"Whom not having seen ye love; on whom, though now ye see him not, yet believing, ye rejoice greatly with joy unspeakable and full of glory" (1 Peter 1.8). Here we are told that we love Him because we have believed in Him. What comes out of such love as a result of faith? There is produced a joy which is unspeakable and full of glory.

In closing I would like to quote the parting word of an elderly man to a young man: May you ever be an ardent lover of the Lord Jesus!

9 | Mary Magdalene

Now on the first day of the week cometh Mary Magdalene early, while it was yet dark, unto the tomb, and seeth the stone taken away from the tomb. She runneth therefore, and cometh to Simon Peter, and the other disciple whom Jesus loved, and saith unto them, They have taken away the Lord out of the tomb, and we know not where they have laid him. Peter therefore went forth, and the other disciple, and they went toward the tomb. And they ran both together: and the other disciple outran Peter, and came first to the tomb; and stooping and looking in, he seeth the linen cloths lying; yet entered he not in. Simon Peter therefore also cometh, following him, and entered into the tomb; and he beholdeth the linen cloths lying, and the napkin, that was upon his head, not lying with the linen cloths, but rolled up in a place by itself. Then entered in therefore the other disciple also, who came first to the tomb, and he saw, and believed. For as yet they knew not the scripture, that he must rise again from the dead. So the disciples went away again unto their own home.

But Mary was standing without at the tomb weeping: so, as she wept, she stooped and looked into the tomb; and she beholdeth two angels in white sitting, one at the head, and one at the feet, where the body of Jesus had lain. And they say unto her, Woman, why weepest thou? She saith unto them, Because they have taken away my Lord, and I know not where they have laid him. When she had thus said, she turned herself back, and beholdeth Jesus standing, and knew not that it was Jesus. Jesus saith unto her, Woman, why weepest thou? whom seekest thou? She, supposing him to be the gardener, saith unto him, Sir, If thou hast borne him hence, tell me where thou hast laid him, and I will take him away. Jesus saith unto her, Mary. She turneth herself, and saith unto him in Hebrew, Rabboni; which is to say, Teacher. Jesus saith unto her, Touch me not; for I am not yet ascended unto the Father: but go unto my brethren and say to them, I ascend unto my Father and your Father, and my God and your God. Mary Magdalene cometh and telleth the disciples, I have seen the Lord; and that he had said these things unto her. (John 20.1–18).

After He had been raised from the dead, the Lord Jesus appeared to many people. But to whom did He appear first? To Mary Magdalene. The Lord was anxious to appear to Peter, for the latter was in great weakness. He was more anxious, however, to appear to Mary Magdalene. He was eager to appear to the two disciples on their way to Emmaus because they had gone the wrong way. Yet he was more eager to appear to Mary Magdalene. He was keen to appear to John, for John was the one whom He loved; but He was keener still to appear to Mary Magdalene. He also was desirous to appear to Thomas due to the latter's unbelief; He was even more desirous to appear to Mary Magdalene. The Lord did in fact appear to many other disciples; nonetheless, He appeared to Mary Magdalene first. Why did He set aside Peter, John, Thomas and all the other disciples and appear first to Mary Magdalene?

One

Please note that Mary Magdalene was the last to leave Calvary's cross and was the first to arrive at the tomb. She was not the only one saved, nor was it from her alone that demons were cast out; yet early in the morning she came to the tomb to find the Lord. True, there were many things she did not understand (some have even thought she did not have a very good brain), but she had a very excellent spiritual portion—one that perhaps many of us lack—which was, that she had a desire for the Lord. This is what every Christian ought to desire after.

It is recorded in John 1.29 that when John the Baptist saw Jesus coming to him, he cried out, "Behold, the Lamb of God, that taketh away the sin of the world!" This is the word which John the Baptist declared when he saw the Lord on that first occasion. Then in verse 36 we read that he saw the Lord

Jesus again and declared: "Behold, the Lamb of God!" Did he forget to finish his sentence with the other words previously uttered ("that taketh away the sin of the world")? No, for this explains the experience of a saved person. When a person first sees the Lord, he invariably thinks of the Lord and himself, of the Lord as the Lamb of God who takes away his sins. But at the second encounter with the Lord, he forgets all about himself and thinks only of the Lord. On the first occasion, he thanks the Lord for the grace given to him; on the second, he draws near to the Lord because of what He is. In baptism, we are joined to the Lord; but in breaking bread, we remember the Lord himself. At our first encounter, we become believers in the Lord; at our second encounter, we become His "sweethearts." The first step is to believe in the work of the Lord; the second step is to draw near to the person of the Lord.

Many there are who only know the preciousness of the Lord's work and do not know the preciousness of the Lord himself. They know the grace they receive, but they do not know the loveliness of the Lord. What makes Mary Magdalene different from other people is that she treasures the Savior himself, not just the salvation she receives.

Many people there are from whom demons are cast out, but one alone seeks after the Lord—even Mary Magdalene. Though other women also came to find the Lord, the first one who arrived at the tomb was Mary Magdalene. She came early on the first day of the week, while it was yet dark. She cared for nothing but finding the Lord. Well has one brother said this, that after the Lord Jesus died, the whole world in Mary's eyes had become a vacuum! The whole world could not at all bewitch her heart, because one person alone had already captivated her. Her heart was fully possessed by the Lord.

Two

When Mary came to the tomb, what did she see? And what did she intend to do? She thought that since her beloved Lord was now dead it would be good if she could see His body once more. Yet unexpectedly, even the body was gone! So she ran to tell Peter and John, saying, "They have taken away the Lord out of the tomb, and we know not where they have laid him." Immediately the two took off and ran to the tomb. John ran faster than Peter, so he arrived at the tomb first. He looked into it and saw the linen cloths lying there, but he did not enter in. Simon Peter arrived afterwards and entered into the tomb and saw the linen cloths lying, also the napkin that had been upon Jesus' head now rolled up in a place by itself. Then John also went in. He saw and believed. Yet what did they do after they had seen the situation? These two "went away again unto their own home." They still had a sweet home on earth to which they could go. Although they realized the absence of the Lord, they felt strongly they should return to their own house. Apart from the Lord, they still had a place to call their home.

How about Mary? "But Mary was standing without at the tomb weeping." She had no place to go!

She could not go! How profound is this word "but"! Mary pondered in her heart: "You may have a home to go to, but I cannot go because the Lord is gone. You may not miss the Lord's presence, but I do. Who has taken Him away? How can I leave?" So that she stood by the tomb and wept. To her, the whole world was all emptiness. The Lord was gone; what else, then, could one do but weep. Oh, Mary's heart is the heart of a widow! The disciples who had followed the Lord could go away. Those with deep knowledge of the Lord could go away. John who loved the Lord went away; the "courageous" Peter also went away. Only a simple woman out of whom the Lord had cast seven demons was captivated by the Lord. She had neither rest nor consolation. She could not go away. Without the Lord all was finished. She could only weep, because thereafter her heart was nothing but a great void.

Three

"So, as she wept, she stooped and looked into the tomb; and she beholdeth two angels in white sitting, one at the head, and one at the feet, where the body of Jesus had lain. And they say unto her, Woman, why weepest thou? She saith unto them, Because they have taken away my Lord, and I know not where they have laid him." When Mary saw the angels, she was neither surprised nor frightened. Why? Because her heart was completely occupied with "they have taken away my Lord." With this one thing in mind, she cared for nothing else. Such a heart was so singularly fixed on her Lord that even the appearance of the angels could not attract her attention. She was not concerned about the angels; her whole heart was focused on the Lord.

Some may feel how good it would be if they could travel along for a while with John who so loved the Lord, or how exciting it might be if they could hear just once the preaching of Peter who was so deeply disciplined by the Lord. But the heart of Mary does not care for such things. To her, the presence of Peter and John is not sufficient for her. For her heart is like the heart of a widow. People may imagine how joyous Mary must have become in having the angels speak to her; but the fact of the matter is she did not feel anything special at all. How very different from men these angels must have appeared; they must have been very attractive, and their garments were white and shining; nevertheless, Mary could only think of one thing: how her Lord had been taken away. Even the resplendent angels could not fill the void of her heart.

There was only one thing she could do, and that was to weep. Without the Lord, nothing could satisfy her, not Peter, not John, not even the angels!

Four

"Woman, why weepest thou?" asked the angels. "Because they have taken away my Lord," she replied, "and I know not where they have laid him." In her thinking, though the Lord had died, His body was still precious. She had not thought of the Lord's resurrection. Four times as recorded in the Gospel according to Matthew, the Lord had told His disciples that after He died He would be raised from among the dead (16.21, 17.23, 20.19, 26.32). Yet Mary knew nothing of it. So that on that day all her hope had been shattered; and then she only desired after the Lord's body. Yet in spite of her ignorance, the Lord revealed himself to her because of her singular desire for Him.

The Lord appeared to Mary so as to satisfy a heart that was hungering and thirsting after Him. Peter and John went home, and the Lord did not seek them out. But here was a heart wholly occupied with the Lord, and hence He sought her out. Let me say that it is not that detrimental if we are somewhat lacking in knowledge; but to have a heart that will stir up the Lord is most precious.

Five

"When she had thus said, she turned herself back, and beholdeth Jesus standing, and knew not that it was Jesus. Jesus saith unto her, Woman, why weepest thou? whom seekest thou? She, supposing him to be the gardener, saith unto him, Sir, if thou hast borne him hence, tell me where thou hast laid him, and I will take him away." She saw the Lord Jesus, but she thought He was the gardener. "Sir, if thou hast borne *him* hence." Here she forgot to state that she was seeking the Lord—Jesus of Nazareth. She merely said "him." To her, there was only "him" in the whole world. She thought everybody ought to know who the "him" was to her. She assumed that everyone should know who this "him" was! And such was the heart of Mary.

"Let him kiss me with the kisses of his mouth"—so begins chapter 1 verse 2 of the Song of Solomon. This was spoken by the Shulammite as an expression of her desire for Solomon. In a similar way, whom Mary desired in her heart was this "Him" and whom she spoke about was also this "Him." How we also need to have this "Him" in our hearts. It is not so important to have spiritual knowledge; having "Him" is all that really matters. We do not need more knowledge; we need such a perfect heart before Him as Mary Magdalene had.

Six

"If thou hast borne him hence, tell me where thou hast laid him, and I will take him away." What kind of person was Mary? She was but a woman. We do not know whether she was physically strong or weak, but we do know that her heart's intention was to take the Lord away herself. At this moment, she had given no thought as to whether she had enough strength or whether the road were too long. She only thought of taking Him. Love knows no difficulty. One quite amazing thing in the world is that where there is love, there is no problem. She was not mindful of anything other than to take Him. And such was the heart of Mary Magdalene.

Confronted by such a state as this, the Lord could not but reveal himself to her. He could not let her weep on. He must satisfy this longing heart and appear to Mary before He could them seek out Peter, John, and the two disciples on the road to Emmaus.

Seven

How did the Lord appear to her? "Jesus saith unto her, Mary. She turneth herself, and saith unto him in Hebrew, Rabboni; which is to say, Teacher." Have we ever heard this voice that Mary heard? If we ever hear this voice—"Mary"—when we pray in our closet, we shall be satisfied. As soon as the Lord said "Mary," she recognized Him right away. This is a revelation. It is enough if the Lord would say but one word. As the shepherd calls his sheep, the eyes of the sheep open immediately. When Mary heard the Lord's voice, she knew instantly that this was not the gardener, but the Teacher. She therefore had no need to weep any more. Whenever the Lord reveals himself to a person, no further words need to be said. Do we, like Mary, recognize the voice of our Lord?

There was once a family which was composed of only two persons, a mother and her son. Every evening when the son came home on his bicycle, he whistled as he approached the house. His mother knew immediately that her son was coming home. One day a brother in the Lord was talking with her at her home. Just as he was leaving, the mother stopped him and asked him to wait for a while, for her son was coming home. Upon inquiring how she knew this, she replied that she had already heard her son's whistle. To other people, the whistle meant nothing, but to the mother's ears it had a special meaning. When the Lord said "Mary," it might not mean anything to others, but Mary recognized this voice and knew it was the Lord.

Eight

"Jesus saith to her, Touch me not; for I am not yet ascended unto the Father: but go unto my brethren, and say to them, I ascend unto my Father and your Father, and my God and your God." In Matthew 28 it is recorded that some women touched the Lord. He allowed them to do so because it was worship. But why did He forbid Mary to touch Him here? Because the Lord knew that Mary wanted to keep the Lord on earth by clinging to Him and would refuse to let Him go. Yet what had the Lord gotten while on earth? Nothing except a thorny crown, a cross, and a tomb. Now He was to ascend to heaven—to His Father and also our Father, to His God and also our God. Hence He told Mary not to touch Him, that is to say, not to detain Him on earth. For the Lord has not only been resurrected, He has also ascended to heaven to be the Head of a new race as well as the representative of men.

Never before had there been any man in heaven. In His ascension, the Lord Jesus became the first man in heaven, and after Him there will be those others who believe in Him. "Because of the suffering of death crowned with glory and honor, . . . for whom are all things, and through whom are all things, in bringing many sons unto glory" (Heb. 2.9,10).

Because of the suffering of death, the Lord is now crowned with glory and honor, and He will lead many other sons into glory too. The Lord has gone ahead, and thereafter the disciples will follow. After His resurrection, He will begin to call the disciples brethren. In other words, the Lord is now the firstborn Son and we become the many sons. By His resurrection and ascension, His Father becomes our Father, and His God becomes our God.

Nine

What more could Mary say? Nothing, for she was truly satisfied. Hence, she went back, because now she *could* go back. Can we ever blame the Lord if we are lacking in such revelation as Mary experienced in seeing and hearing Him? Absolutely not, because it can only be due to our lack of hunger and thirst for the Lord that Mary had. Let us ask ourselves if we really long for the Lord? Do we desire the Son of God with all our heart? Are we ignorant of the fact that our position or fame cannot at all touch the Lord's heart, but that He will be touched if we really yearn after Him? May God create such a desire in us so that we may desire after the Son of God and love Him with singleness of heart.